LEARN TO SING
STEP BY STEP
By Ronny Lee

Ronny Lee is the author of more than eighty music instruction books which are sold throughout the world. Also, he has written popular, classical and rock arrangements for various publishers. These include *Man of La Mancha, The Sound of Music,* and the Beatles' *A Hard Day's Night.*

His articles on all aspects of music and the business of making music have appeared in trade and consumer publications. He has conducted workshops and seminars for music teachers, and has officiated as adjudicator at major music festivals.

A musician, teacher, writer and singer who is knowledgeable in all styles of music, Ronny Lee has performed on literally thousands of engagements. These include club dates, recording sessions and appearances with the New York Philharmonic.

Thanks to my good friend, Raymond Sabinsky, violist with the New York Philharmonic and life-long student of voice, who was a source of much valuable information which he generously imparted to me.

Edited by Frances Lee

SUNRISE PUBLISHING
COMPANY, INCORPORATED
P.O. BOX 408 • NEW YORK, N.Y. 10019

TABLE OF CONTENTS

PRELUDE

THE SINGING VOICE AND ITS PRODUCTION

The fundamentals of singing are relatively easy to understand. In fact, almost anyone can learn to sing.

The singing voice is a musical instrument that is capable of modulating its tones with words. The four parts of the vocal instrument are (1) the lungs, which supply the flow of air; (2) the vocal cords, which produce the sound; (3) the resonance cavities, which amplify the sound; and (4) the organs of speech, which superimpose words on the tones produced by the vocal cords.

The lungs supply the flow of air which passes between the vocal cords, causing them to vibrate. The barely audible sounds of the vocal cords are amplified by the resonance cavities of the body—namely the chest, throat, mouth, nose and sinus cavities of the head—and modulated by words formed in the mouth.

The singing voice is produced in the same manner as the speaking voice. However, the singing voice offers considerably greater variation in pitch and its tones are sustained for longer periods. Also, the singing voice may be produced with vibrato.

THE VOCAL CORDS

The vocal cords are two strips of cartilage, roughly a half inch in length in a man and less in a woman or child. During the intake of breath, the cords are wide apart. To produce sound they come together, narrowing the passage separating them. When air is forced between the vocal cords they vibrate, permitting puffs of air to pass. The greater the frequency of the puffs of air, the higher the pitch of the tone produced. For high notes, the cords increase their tension and vibrate rapidly. For low notes, the cords become slack and vibrate slowly.

The vocal cords provide pitch (highness or lowness of tone). When we whisper, the vocal cords are apart and are not used; the tongue, lips, teeth and other speech organs shape the air into words as it leaves the mouth. When we hum, the vocal cords are responsible for production of variously pitched tones; the organs of speech are not used.

THE RESONANCE CAVITIES

The resonance cavities (chest, throat, mouth, nose and sinus cavities) provide amplification and quality to the voice. The vocal cords may be compared to the strings on a violin. The resonance cavities may be compared to the body of the violin.

POSTURE

Before one learns to play an instrument, one should learn how to hold it. Applied to the singer, this means POSTURE.

There is unanimous agreement among vocal experts that good posture is a necessity for good singing. Good posture allows the inhalation and expiration of breath with the least effort. Good posture is conducive to greater freedom for the body cavities to perform their function as resonance chambers. If the posture is good, the body can maintain a greater state of relaxation. There is no doubt that good posture is an important ingredient in the mixture required for good voice production.

The ideal singing posture is attained while standing. The spine should be straight and the body relaxed. Never should the singer assume the stance of the soldier at attention. Relaxation is the key word.

Frequently it is necessary for the singer to be seated. The same rules of posture apply when seated. The spine is to be straight and the body relaxed. The body is never to be slumped or hunched forward.

BREATHING

We speak loudly to be heard above the din. We speak softly to avoid waking the baby. We speak tenderly to those we love. We speak angrily when we are annoyed. We speak quickly when we are excited. We speak slowly when we offer instructions to a foreigner. We speak long phrases. We speak a single syllable. And, despite the varying circumstances under which we speak, we are never conscious of our breathing.

By breathing naturally when we speak, we allow the breathing process to take care of itself. If we should attempt to control our breathing when speaking, like inhaling at the beginning of each sentence, the act of breathing would pose numerous problems. These problems are eliminated merely by letting our body and subconscious mind take care of the breathing for us.

In general, the inhalation of breath while singing should be accomplished in the same manner as when sleeping. During the intake of air the abdomen should expand. There should be little if any motion of the upper chest during inhalation. When singing, breath should be taken in through the mouth because it is faster and easier. At times, breath may be taken in through the nose when it feels more natural to inhale in this manner. Other than breathing through the mouth, breathing when singing is to be treated the same as breathing when speaking. Then it will never pose a problem.

The less the singer concentrates on specific muscular actions when breathing, the less distracted he will be.

BREATH CONTROL

The term "BREATH CONTROL" refers to control over the amount of air expended in order to perform long passages of music on a single breath.

The concept of breath control spawns the question, "Why is it necessary to sing long passages on a single breath?" Though the tempo of a selection has a bearing upon breathing, the singer can always find an appropriate place at which to breathe, long before running out of breath.

For example, if the phrase "I came, I saw, I conquered" is spoken (or sung) quickly, the complete phrase is performed on a single breath. If the phrase is spoken (or sung) very slowly, breaths may be taken where the commas occur. If the phrase is spoken (or sung) at a moderate pace, a breath may be taken at the point of either one of the two commas. Breathing and phrasing have little effect upon each other. Phrases are the result of pauses that occur in conversation (or a lyric). And, as in conversation, breaths can be taken at various appropriate times without affecting phrasing.

As for developing the ability to sing long passages on a single breath, this is acquired by practicing vocal exercises.

IMAGERY

Despite the richness of language, there exist sensations which are beyond the realm of description. Imagine the futility in attempting to describe the color "blue" to a blind man, or the taste of a tomato to a person who has never before heard of this plant. Can the smell of bacon frying, the touch of cellophane, or the sound of ocean waves be accurately described to someone who has never experienced these sensations? Think how difficult it is merely to describe the act of swallowing.

In a nutshell, we are unable to describe the sensations of taste, smell, sight, sound and touch to anyone who has not experienced the sensation we are describing. And for that reason it is not possible to describe to a student the physical sensations a singer is to feel to produce properly a high-pitched note or a low-pitched note or a mid-range note.

Because of this, voice teachers use imagery as a means of communication. Some commonly used examples of imagery are: (1) Sing on top of the breath. (2) Support the tone. (3) Spin out the notes. (4) Sing with a warm tone. (5) Make the tone rise from the feet. (6) Focus the tone. (7) Shape the throat like a pear. (8) Make it sound like maple syrup.

At times, the student may be told to direct the stream of sound towards one part of the anatomy or another, although this is physically impossible.

When imagery is used, words commonly employed to describe tone are: focused, deep, pointed, round, forward, back, cool, warm, bright, dark, gleeful, gloomy, velvet, honey. Unfortunately, none of these words provide a specific meaning or directive to the student.

Because the image in the teacher's mind may appear as something totally different in the mind of the student, much confusion often arises from the use of imagery. Even students of the same teacher may have different interpretations for the same imagery.

Despite its shortcomings as a teaching device, it is possible for the student to benefit by using imagery upon himself. By thinking of velvet or honey, he may be able to influence the quality of his tone.

SUPPORTING THE VOICE

Perhaps no example of imagery has been bandied about by voice teachers as much as that of "supporting the voice." One writer claims that mastery of voice production is impossible unless the student has first learned to "support the voice." The same writer goes on to state that the voice is to be supported by the breath as though it is a ping pong ball supported by air.

It is not unusual for a voice teacher to shout at his student during the performance of a vocal exercise or a song to "support the voice."

The truth of the matter is that the suggestion to "support the voice" has no meaning. If it suggests that the voice is somehow supported by the breath, this is not possible because the voice *is* the breath.

The four components of the vocal instrument are the lungs, the vocal cords, the resonance cavities, and the speech organs. Nowhere in this chain does voice support (whatever that means) have any bearing upon voice production.

It is interesting that a phrase so frequently used defies being uniformly defined by its users.

EXPERTS DIFFER ON THE IDEAL PLACEMENT OF THE VOICE

There is divided opinion among experts regarding where the voice is to be placed. Many experts believe that for proper placement, the singer should feel the tone in BOTH the chest and the head at the same time. The singer should feel that the high-pitched tone, which is placed mainly in the head, is also directing some vibration toward the chest, thereby acquiring some of the warmth of the chest resonance.* Conversely, the low-pitched tone, which is placed mainly in the chest, should acquire some of the brilliance of the head resonance.

Other experts believe that the singer should place the voice up and forward, so the physical sensation is that of the voice bouncing off the palate and projecting forward, much like sound bouncing off a band shell.

And still other experts believe that all of the above will take place naturally, without any conscious effort of voice placement, provided the singer can maintain total relaxation while singing.

PLACING THE VOICE

To PLACE THE VOICE is to direct the *feeling* of vibration to a particular location of the resonance cavities. In reality, it is impossible to direct the stream of sound towards one part of the anatomy or another. The illusion that the voice has been placed at a specific area, such as the chest or head, grows out of the real sensations of sympathetic vibration.

When singing a mellow, low-pitched tone, the vibration (placement) is felt in the chest. The tone feels as though it is directed (placed) down and back. A brilliant high-pitched tone is felt (placed) in the head. It appears to be directed (placed) up and forward.

By thinking it so, the low-pitched tone can be placed in the head, while the high-pitched tone can be placed in the chest. Since the placement of the voice is accomplished in the mind, the singer may influence his tone by thinking of the resonance area(s) to which he would like to direct his voice.

It is through trial and error that the student learns the best positions for the vocal organs and the placement that will provide the best results.

THE OPEN THROAT

An important function of vocal exercises is to enable the student to sing with an open throat. Unless the throat is fully opened while singing, it is unlikely that the maximum potential of the voice will be realized.

Unfortunately, it is no more possible for the beginner to maintain an open position of the throat than it is to control his blood pressure.

When a physician wishes to examine his patient's throat, he tells him to say "AH." During the utterance of this syllable, the throat is wide open. It is for this reason that the syllable "AH" plays a prominent role in the vocal exercises which follow.

To relax the throat and to further assure its open position, it is recommended that the student think of yawning while singing "AH."

After a few months of vocalizing using the syllable "AH," the open position of the throat will become natural. At that point other syllables will be introduced. When singing these syllables, the student will attempt to maintain the same open position of the throat as is employed for the syllable "AH."

---

* In common usage, the word "register" is often used instead of "resonance." For example, reference may be made to the "chest register" or the "head register."

THE PHYSIOLOGICAL APPROACH TO SINGING

Most of the great singing teachers claim that the less one knows about the physiology of singing, the better. They argue that one need not be familiar with the numerous muscles and tendons involved with playing the violin in order to become an accomplished violinist.

An excellent singing teacher who had a vast knowledge of the physiological aspects of singing was Manuel Garcia.

Manuel Garcia (1805-1906) was a singing teacher and vocal expert of supereminent reputation. Also, he acquired fame as the inventor of the laryngoscope in 1855. This device permitted scientists to study the functions and actions of the vocal cords, and made possible the accumulation of knowledge valuable to physiologists and phoneticians.

Charles Santley (1834-1922) was the greatest British baritone of his day and a student of Manuel Garcia.

Santley wrote in his book *(The Art of Singing),* "Manuel Garcia is held up as the pioneer of scientific (mechanistic) teachers of singing. He was—but he taught singing, not surgery! I was a pupil of his in 1858, and a friend of his while he lived (to 1906), and in all the conversation I had with him, I never heard him say a word about larynx or pharynx, glottis, or other organ used in the production and emission of the voice."

THE BEAT OF MUSIC

In all music there is a beat or pulse which prevails from the beginning of a selection until the very end. Whether there are two, three, or four beats to the bar, this musical heartbeat is constantly present. The beat, whether it is heard or only felt, is what we tap our foot to or clap our hands to when listening to music.

TEMPO

In a musical selection or study, the speed with which the beats follow each other is called the TEMPO. Tempo may be fast, slow, or anywhere in between.

THE METRONOME

A metronome is a device which either mechanically or electrically emits a continuous series of evenly spaced clicks at a rate established by the positioning of a counterweight on a rod or pointer on a dial. The metronome enables the performer to duplicate exactly the tempo of a selection or exercise merely by setting the metronome indicator to match the metronome marks appearing on the music sheet.

READING THE METRONOME MARK

The metronome mark contains a note and a number. The note that is shown receives one beat. The number represents the amount of clicks (beats) sounded each minute. For example, ♩ = 96 means that the quarter note is played at the rate of ninety-six to the minute; ♩ = 72 means that the quarter note is played at the rate of seventy-two to the minute, etc.

For the beginner who is unfamiliar with music notation, this will become clear after only a few weeks of study from the MUSIC THEORY section of this book.

The metronome was invented by Johann Nepomuk Maelzel (1772-1838), a friend of Beethoven. It is interesting to note that it was Maelzel who invented the eàr trumpet, which was so useful to Beethoven at the time he was losing his hearing.

In recognition of Maelzel's invention of the metronome, the metronome mark was formerly written M.M. ♩ = 96. The initials M.M., which stand for Maelzel's Metronome, are now omitted.

THE IMPORTANCE OF METRONOME MARKS TO THE VOICE STUDENT

Because the difficulty encountered when singing high-pitched notes is directly proportional to the time allotted to them, the metronome marks appearing in the section, DEVELOPING THE VOICE, are relevant and must be observed.

IMPORANT RULES FOR WARMING UP AND VOCALIZING

1. Vocal exercises are to be practiced every day. During the early stages, practice periods are not to exceed 15 minutes. If possible, the student should practice several times a day. As the voice grows stronger, the practice periods are to be extended.

2. Never strain the voice. If strain is felt or if the voice grows tired, stop practicing until the voice feels rested. Yawning is good medicine when the voice feels strained.

3. Try to be as relaxed as possible. Relaxation is one of the most important qualities for good singing.

4. For the best tone production with the least effort, stand with good posture. Don't slump. If it is necessary to be seated while singing, sit up straight. Don't be stiff or assume the posture of a soldier standing at attention.

5. If the throat feels dry, try swallowing a few times or drink some water.

6. Dizziness sometimes occurs when vocalizing. If this should happen, rest for a moment and then resume practice. In time, the dizziness will no longer appear.

7. Breathe in through the mouth—except when it feels more comfortable to breathe in through the nose.

8. Assume a pleasant facial expression with just a hint of a smile. Don't attempt a broad smile or grin from ear to ear, as this produces an unpleasant tone quality.

9. For each tone that is produced, think of being on the verge of yawning. This insures an open, relaxed throat.

10. For as long as voice is studied, it is necessary to begin with the warmup (shown on page 8) before proceeding with the vocal exercises.

11. Begin the warmup softly. Continue at this low volume level until the voice is warmed up. Then sing at a comfortable level of volume. Never force the voice. Over a period of time, the voice will develop more than enough power from practicing at a moderate volume.

12. Never attempt to sing notes that are so high or so low that strain is placed upon the throat. A broad range is developed by vocalizing notes that can be sung without strain.

13. The warmup and vocal exercises are to be practiced with instrumental accompaniment to assure proper intonation.*

14. The warmup is to be practiced without vibrato. If the pupil wishes, vibrato may be applied to sustained notes that appear in the vocal exercises.

15. The jaw should be relaxed, loose and free of rigidity. This can be attained by imagining total relaxation in the cheek muscles below the eyes.

---

* If you do not play an instrument nor have an accompanist, cassette tape #RL 6942 is available to demonstrate and provide accompaniment for the warmup and vocalises that follow.

THE VOCALISE *(VOH-kah-leez)*

VOCALISE is a word that means "vocal exercise." The vocalise plays a necessary role in developing the singing voice.

The practice of vocalises *(VOH-kah-leez-iz)* may be compared to warmups, exercises and practice activities performed by athletes. While their use does not guarantee that one will become a good athlete (or singer), they provide the tools needed to improve an individual's skill to its fullest potential.

The vocalise enables the singer to improve tone quality and intonation (to sing in tune), increase the vocal range and acquire technique and flexibility. The singer who does not practice vocalises is like the athlete who does not engage in training activities other than the game itself.

The great singing teacher Niccolo Antonio Porpora (1686-1766) taught many singers whose names are famous to this day. It is said that Porpora confined his pupil, Caffarelli, for five years to the vocalises written on a single sheet of paper, and then sent him into the world with the blessing, "Go, my son, I can teach you nothing more. You are the greatest singer in Europe."

UNUSUAL METHODS OF VOICE TRAINING

William Herschel (1738-1822), an organist and composer, was also the voice teacher of his sister, Caroline. The method of vocal training adopted for her was to sing the violin parts of concertos with a gag in her mouth.

Though Caroline had considerable success in Handel's oratorios under her brother's tutelage, one wonders whether her level of vocal ability was acquired because of her unusual training or in spite of it. Granted that such vocal training techniques are laughable and frowned upon by knowledgeable teachers of voice, similarly ridiculous techniques are currently used by misguided voice teachers.

Beware when a voice teacher recommends a surgical operation to remove connective tissue beneath the tongue supposedly to provide greater control of the tongue. Steer clear of a voice teacher who suggests that you repeatedly jab yourself in the chest and abdominal area while sustaining an AH sound, for the purpose of developing a vibrato. Make a hasty retreat from an instructor who suggests that you ask a friend to stand on your chest and abdomen for extended periods of time to develop your breathing muscles. Breathing muscles are properly developed by singing vocalises, and not by gymnastics or feats of strength. In short, discontinue lessons with an instructor who suggests anything which appears to border on the absurd.

LET'S LEARN TO SING

Learning to sing requires a great deal of hard work and a considerable period of time. Occasionally it may be discouraging, and practicing may not be enjoyable, but for those who persevere and eventually develop the glorious voice and singing style they once dreamed about, it is all worth it.

Much like the shipwrecked sailor who builds a boat to escape from an island, the person who would like to sing must also develop the means to escape from the land of the Non-Singers. However, the boat to the land of the Singing People is constructed of vocalises, music theory, ear training, sight singing, and delivery technique.

You are ready to embark. Good luck on your journey.

SECTION ONE

DEVELOPING THE VOICE

The MUSIC THEORY section beginning on page 50 is to be studied concurrently with this section.

DEVELOPING THE VOICE—LESSON ONE

To insure that no strain is placed upon the vocal apparatus, the warmup exercise should always precede the vocalises during the first practice period of each day. If the daily practice periods are widely spaced, it is wise to warm up before each period of practice.

The warmup and vocalises which follow are presented with accompaniment parts. The vocal part appears on the upper staff with the accompaniment part directly below. The accompaniments are written on a simple level, and may be provided by a keyboard instrument, guitar or any chord producing instrument.*

The teacher/accompanist may embellish or modify the accompaniment part. However, it is essential that the single note melody is played together with the vocalise that is sung by the pupil.

Begin singing the warmup softly. Continue at this low volume level until the voice is warmed up. Then sing at a comfortable level of volume. Do not force the voice and do not attempt to sing loudly.

If the voice feels extremely "cold" and on the verge of straining, the warmup exercise should be sung two times at a very low level of volume. This low volume level is to be maintained until the voice feels warmed up, at which time a normal, moderate level of volume may be employed for the vocalise practice.

In the warmup exercise, vocalises, and solmizations that follow, the starting note of each exercise is selected arbitrarily. If a note is too high (or too low) for the voice, the student is to select a starting pitch that lies comfortably within the vocal range. As the vocal range becomes broader, the vocalises are to be extended to accommodate the expanding range.

Air is to be inhaled in a natural, relaxed manner. The student should not attempt to quickly gulp huge amounts of air. The intake of air should be accomplished in a manner very similar to that of inhaling while speaking. A very large reserve of air is unnecessary.

The BREATH MARK is a musical sign that indicates where the singer is to take a breath. Various signs are used to represent the breath mark. The signs are:

, ✓ * V //

Notice that breath marks appear in the Warmup Exercise.

It is not our purpose to make beautiful music at this time. The objective is to become familiar with our vocal apparatus and to pave the way to the development of a voice that can be used on a professional level in the musical field of our choice.

Each lesson is to be practiced for one week before proceeding to the following lesson.

---

* If an instrument is not convenient or feasible, a cassette tape #RL 6942 is available to demonstrate and provide accompaniment for the warmup and vocalises.

Below is the warmup exercise. It is to be performed at the beginning of each practice session for as long as the student studies voice.

WARMUP EXERCISE

(Begin with the lowest comfortable note and ascend to the highest comfortable note. Then descend to the lowest comfortable note.)

THE INTERVAL

Vocalises (1-1) and (1-2) afford vocal practice on the first two notes of the Major scale. In music, the distance from one note to another is called an INTERVAL. The interval from the first note of the scale to the second note of the scale is called "an interval of a second."

THE SLUR

The SLUR is a curved line appearing over or under two or more notes indicating that they are to be sung in a smooth and connected manner with no break between the tones. Slurred notes are to be sung with one breath. Two or more groups of slurred notes may be sung on the same breath without inhaling, though there is a separation between each series.

Another word with the same meaning as the slur is LEGATO *(leh-GAH-toe)*. Notes which are sung legato flow smoothly from one note to the next.

VOCALISE (1-1)

(Begin with the lowest comfortable note and ascend to the highest comfortable note. Then descend to the lowest comfortable note.)

VOCALISE (1-2)

(Begin with the lowest comfortable note and ascend to the highest comfortable note. Then descend to the lowest comfortable note.)

VOCALISE (1-3)

(Begin with the lowest comfortable note and ascend to the highest comfortable note. Then descend to the lowest comfortable note.)

DEVELOPING THE VOICE—LESSON TWO

In this lesson vocalises (2-1) and (2-2) afford practice on the first three notes of the Major scale. The interval from the first note of the scale to the third note of the scale is called "an interval of a third."

Good posture and a relaxed manner are vital to deriving maximum benefits from vocal practice. In addition to the daily practice of the vocalises the student is encouraged to sing his own favorite songs.

Remember that each practice session, for as long as the pupil studies voice, is always to begin with the warmup exercise. Always begin the warmup exercise and each vocalise with the lowest comfortable note, and then ascend to the highest comfortable note. Then descend to the lowest comfortable note.

If phlegm is present on the vocal cords, the warmup, vocalises or gentle singing will often remove it. If the phlegm is persistent, the only sensible cure is to clear the throat. Though frequent clearing of the throat is irritating to the delicate vocal apparatus, occasional clearing of the throat will cause no harm.

If during vocal practice there should be a need to swallow or rest momentarily, the student should not hesitate to do so. The teacher/accompanist will wait until you are ready to continue.

The student may find some notes in the middle of the vocal range that are more difficult to sing than others. If this occurs, sing the troublesome notes gently and free of tension. In time the student will acquire a vocal range that can be sung smoothly and effortlessly from one end to the other; a vocal range free of any vexing notes.

VOCALISE (2-1)

VOCALISE (2-2)

VOCALISE (2-3)

♩= 76
ah
C
C
ah
C♯
C♯
ah
D
D
ah
D♯
D♯
ah
E
E
ah
F
F
ah
F♯
F♯
ah
G
G
ah
G♭
G♭
ah
F
F
ah
E
E
ah
E♭
E♭
ah
D
D
ah
D♭
D♭
ah
C
C

DEVELOPING THE VOICE—LESSON THREE

In this lesson vocalises (3-1) and (3-2) afford practice on the first four notes of the Major scale. The interval from the first note of the scale to the fourth note of the scale is called "an interval of a fourth."

Sing the AH syllable and listen to the sound. Now try opening the mouth a bit more and sing AH again. Is the sound improved? Try singing AH with a broad smile on your face. Notice how the sound suffers. Try singing AH with a pleasant expression on your face. Notice the improvement of your tone. Everyone has a "best position" to produce the best tone. Continue experimenting until you find the "best position" for your mouth, lips and teeth.

It is through trial and error that the vocal student learns the best position of the vocal organs to produce each note most effectively. This knowledge is acquired by continually searching for the best vocal positioning for each note while practicing the vocalises.

Avoid wearing a tight belt or clothing that is snug around the waist, as this prevents the inhalation of a sufficient amount of air.

If the student encounters difficulty in singing, on one breath, the phrase indicated by the slur, the final, sustained note may be abbreviated or the metronome tempo may be increased slightly. If the phrase still cannot be sung on one breath, a sneak breath (short quick breath) may be taken at an appropriate place. The musical sign that indicates a sneak breath (also called a "catch breath") is ✓✗ .

Remember to begin each vocal exercise with the lowest comfortable note and then ascend to the highest comfortable note. Then descend to the lowest comfortable note.

VOCALISE (3-1)

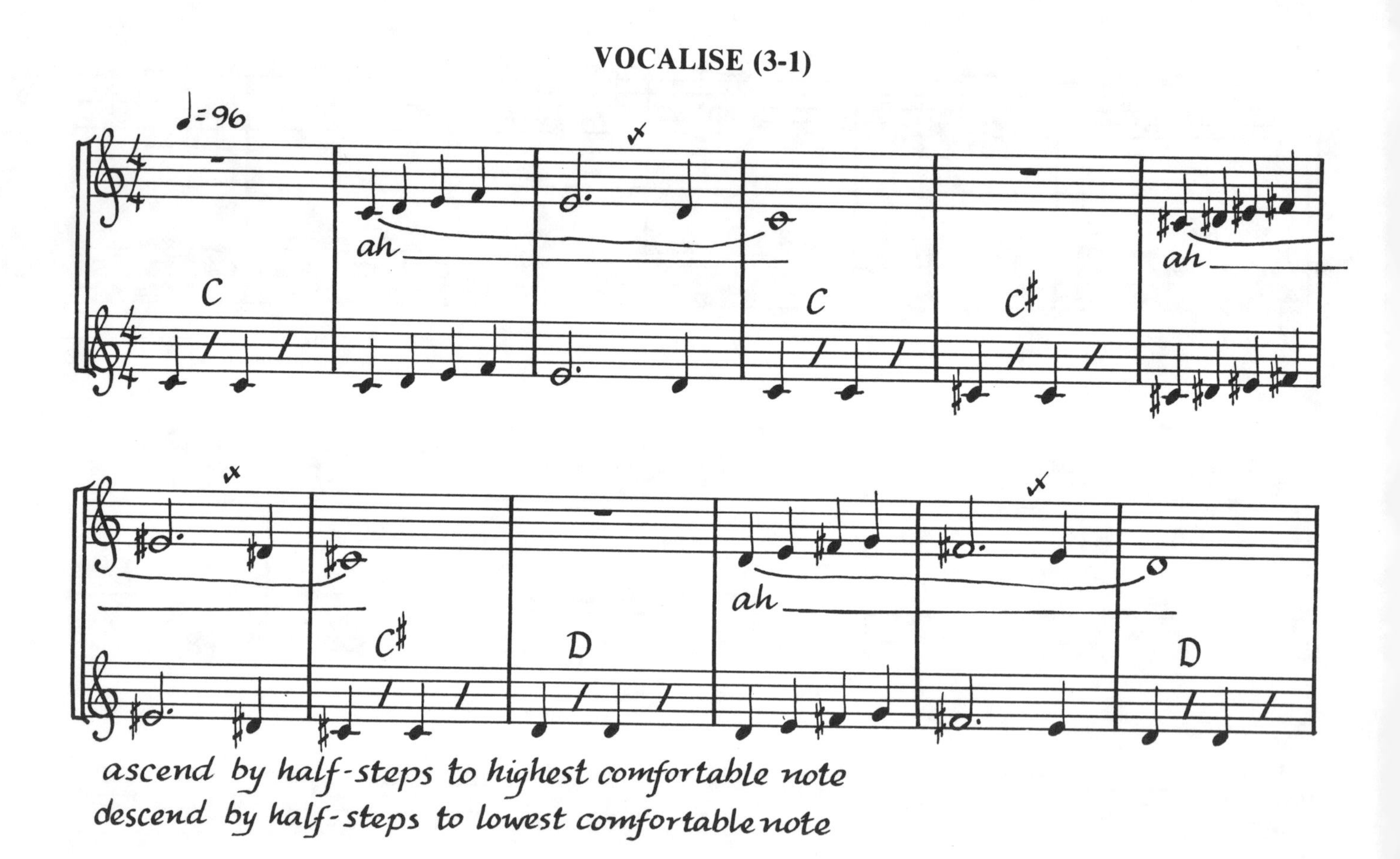

VOCALISE (3-2)

ascend by half-steps to highest comfortable note
descend by half-steps to lowest comfortable note

VOCALISE (3-3)

ascend by half-steps to highest comfortable note
descend by half-steps to lowest comfortable note

DEVELOPING THE VOICE—LESSON FOUR

The vocalises in this lesson afford practice on the first five notes of the Major scale. The interval from the first note of the scale to the fifth note of the scale is called "an interval of a fifth."

When singing, the mind should be absorbed in thought of the sound that is desired.

Attempt to sing the vocalises with feeling, as if each vocalise is a song.

If the student is unable to sing, on one breath, the phrase indicated by the slur, the tempo of the vocalise may be slightly increased and the final note of the phrase may be abbreviated. If the phrase cannot be sung on one breath despite these measures, a catch breath may be taken at an appropriate place.

Begin each vocalise with the lowest comfortable note and then ascend to the highest comfortable note. Then descend to the lowest comfortable note.

VOCALISE (4-1)

VOCALISE (4-2)

VOCALISE (4-3)

DEVELOPING THE VOICE—LESSON FIVE

Vocalises (5-1) and (5-3) appearing in this lesson afford practice on the first six notes of the Major scale. The interval from the first note of the scale to the sixth note of the scale is called "an interval of a sixth."

With continued practice the vocal range will gradually increase.

Greater effort is required for the production of high-pitched notes. This is because the vocal cords grow tauter for high-pitched notes, requiring more force (pressure of air) to set them in motion.

Never attempt to sing any note loudly until it first can properly be sung softly.

If the student is unable to sing, on one breath, the phrase indicated by the slur, the tempo of the vocalise may be slightly increased and/or the final note of the phrase may be abbreviated. If the phrase cannot be sung on one breath despite these measures, a sneak breath may be taken at an appropriate place.

Begin each vocalise with the lowest comfortable note and ascend to the highest comfortable note. Then descend to the lowest comfortable note.

VOCALISE (5-1)

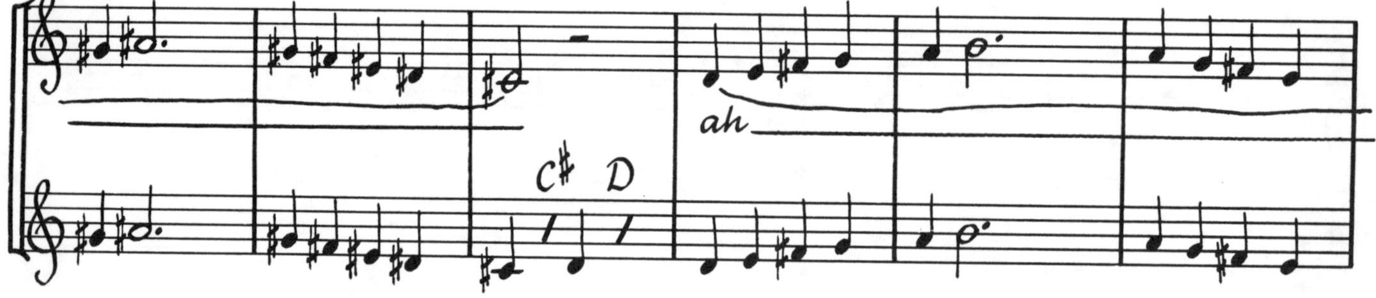

ascend by half-steps to highest comfortable note
descend by half-steps to lowest comfortable note

VOCALISE (5-2)

VOCALISE (5-3)

DEVELOPING THE VOICE—LESSON SIX

The vocalises in this lesson afford practice on the first seven notes of the Major scale. The interval from the first note of the scale to the seventh note of the scale is called "an interval of a seventh."

Though some experts believe that singing is beneficial during a light head cold, under no circumstance should one sing if there is continuous coughing, sore throat, laryngitis or if extremely exhausted.

If the student is unable to sing, on one breath, the phrase indicated by the slur, the tempo of the vocalise may be slightly increased and/or the final note of the phrase may be shortened. If the phrase still cannot be sung on one breath, a sneak breath may be taken at an appropriate place.

All vocal practice should be performed at a soft to moderate level and never with a loud voice. However, there is a practical limit to the degree of softness with which one can sing. A voice that is produced too softly cannot provide the quality of which it is capable. Just as the bicycle rider must maintain a minimum level of speed to maintain balance, so too must the singer vocalize and sing at a level of volume sufficient to maintain a good tone quality.

Begin each vocalise with the lowest comfortable note and ascend to the highest comfortable note. Then descend to the lowest comfortable note.

Remember to precede the daily practice of vocalises with the warmup.

VOCALISE (6-1)

VOCALISE (6-2)

VOCALISE (6-3)

DEVELOPING THE VOICE—LESSON SEVEN

Vocalises (7-1) and (7-3) provide practice on the eight notes that comprise the Major scale. The interval from the first note of the scale to the eighth note of the scale is called "an interval of an octave."

During the preceding lessons the student was becoming acquainted with his vocal equipment. At this point the objective is the production of a beautiful tone. This is accomplished by thinking of a beautiful tone even before the vocal cords are set in motion.

To develop the voice the student must fix in his mind the desired tone. Then he must attempt to produce the tone that is heard in the mind. Learning to sing is as much a matter of developing the mind as it is developing the vocal organs. The vocalises enable the vocal organs to properly respond to the mind.

One way to avoid strain when yelling at sporting events is to ease into the yells. This is accomplished by placing an "H" in front of the vowels. For example, when cheerleaders want you to give them an "A," give them a "HEY" instead. With all the crowd noise no one will know the difference, and you'll be doing your vocal cords a big favor.

Begin each vocalise with the lowest comfortable note and ascend to the highest comfortable note. Then descend to the lowest comfortable note. Use a catch breath if necessary.

Always begin daily vocal practice with the warmup exercise.

VOCALISE (7-1)

VOCALISE (7-2)

VOCALISE (7-3)

DEVELOPING THE VOICE—LESSON EIGHT

The vocalises in lesson eight afford practice on the nine notes that comprise the repeated Major scale. The interval from the first note of the scale to the ninth note of the scale is called "an interval of a ninth."

Never sing fast, technical passages loudly. These are to be sung lightly.

Lower pitched notes are to be sung with less volume than notes in the mid or upper ranges of the voice. This is to avoid placing strain on the vocal cords.

Not only does the warmup exercise limber up the voice for the singing of vocalises, but the daily warmup provides practice in the singing of sustained tones (long tones). This is excellent training for expiring the breath at a steady, even, measured rate—a requisite for good tone quality and the elimination of shortness of breath.

Begin each vocalise with the lowest comfortable note and ascend to the highest comfortable note. Then descend to the lowest comfortable note. Use a sneak breath if necessary.

VOCALISE (8-1)

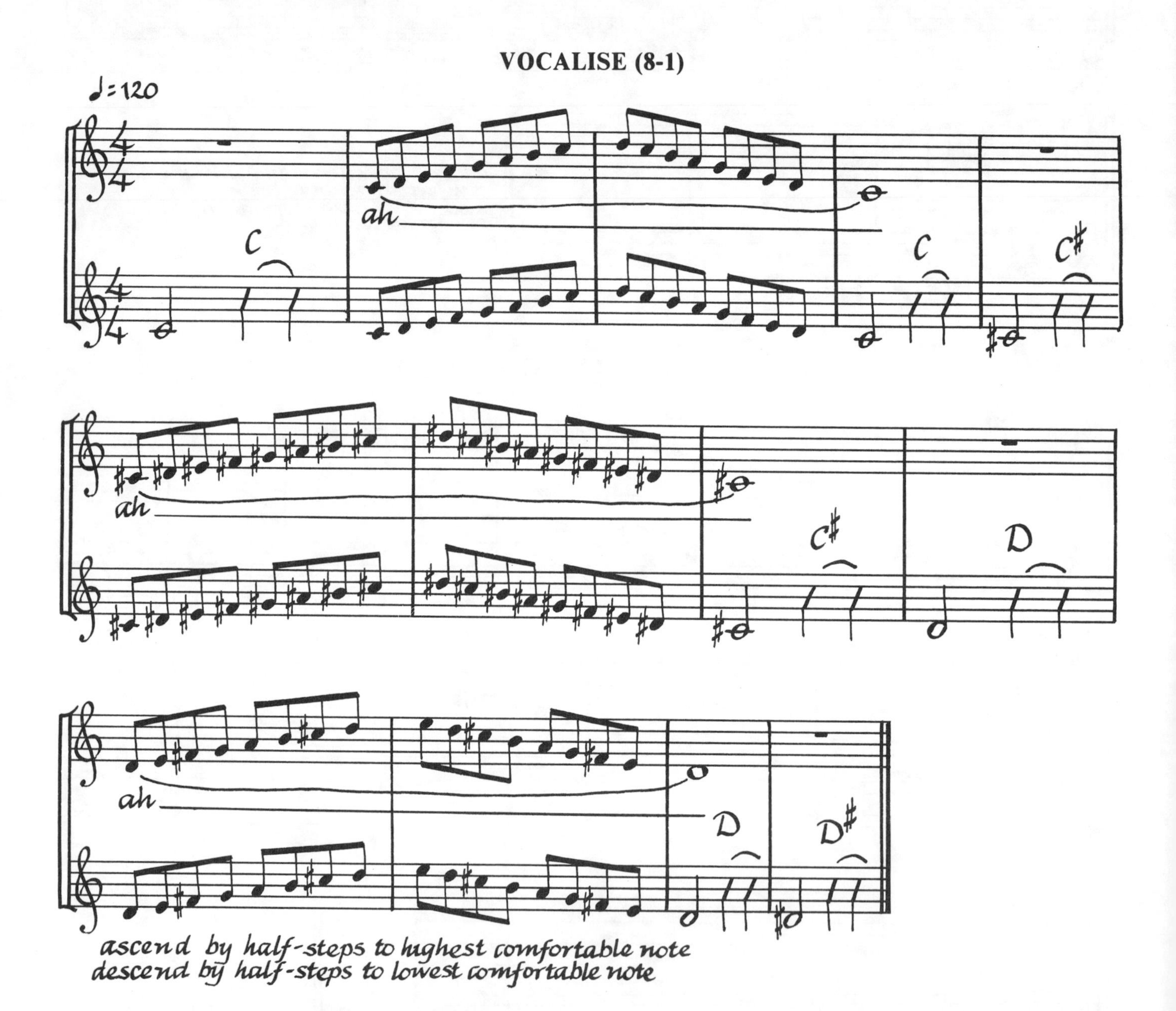

VOCALISE (8-2)

ascend by half-steps to highest comfortable note
descend by half-steps to lowest comfortable note

VOCALISE (8-3)

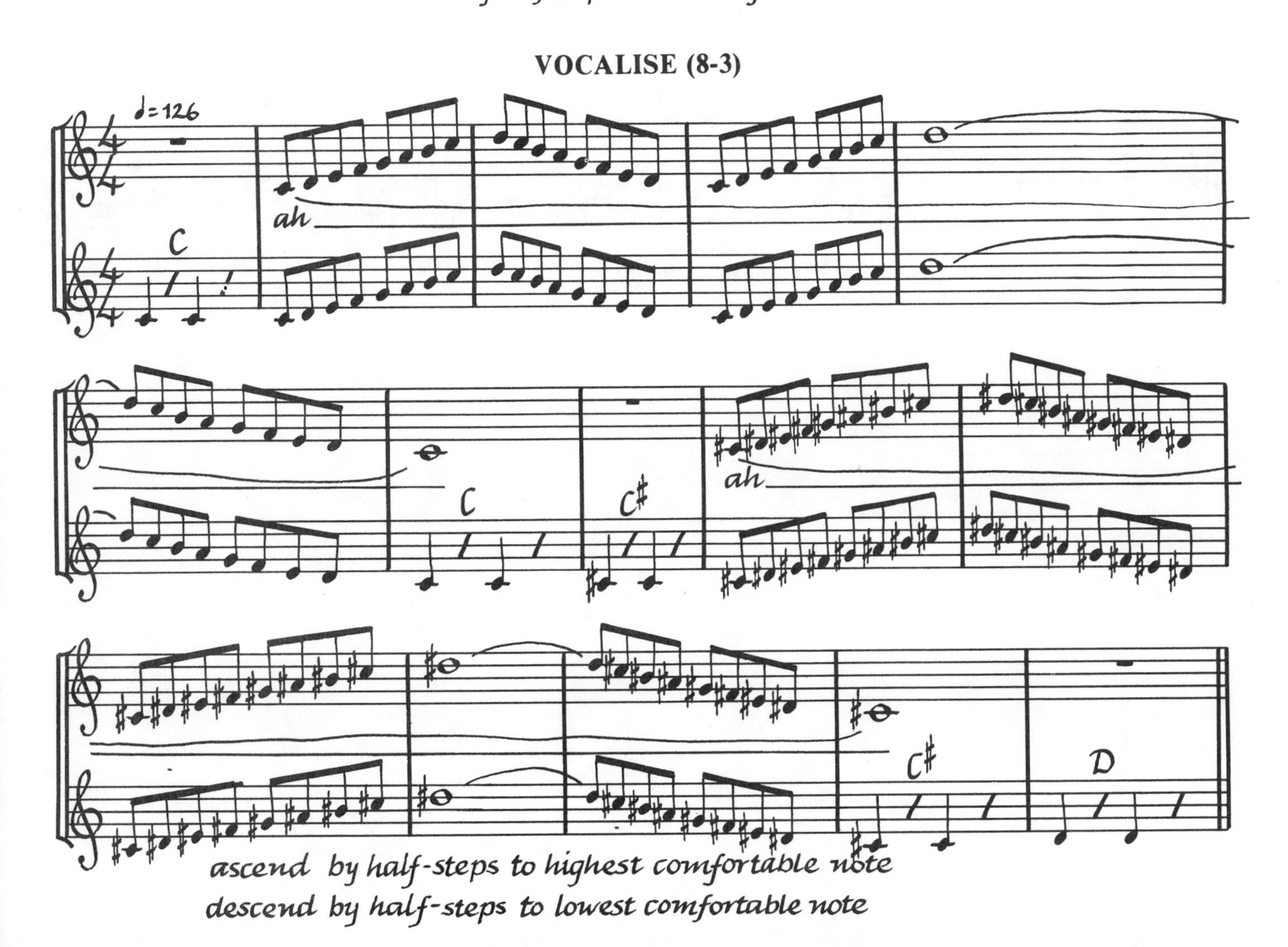

DEVELOPING THE VOICE—LESSON NINE

The vocalises in this lesson afford practice on two scalewise passages. The first passage, which spans an interval of a fifth, is followed by a scalewise movement that spans an interval of a ninth.

Do not tilt the head upward when singing high tones, or downward when singing low tones. This creates tension, which is the singer's archenemy.

Every singer has a "best position" for each vowel sound. For example, one singer may prefer to open the mouth very wide when singing "AH," while another may favor a mouth opening that is not as wide.

Begin each vocalise with the lowest comfortable note and ascend to the highest comfortable note. Then descend to the lowest comfortable note.

Notice the sneak breath sign appearing in vocalises (9-2) and (9-3).

VOCALISE (9-1)

VOCALISE (9-2)

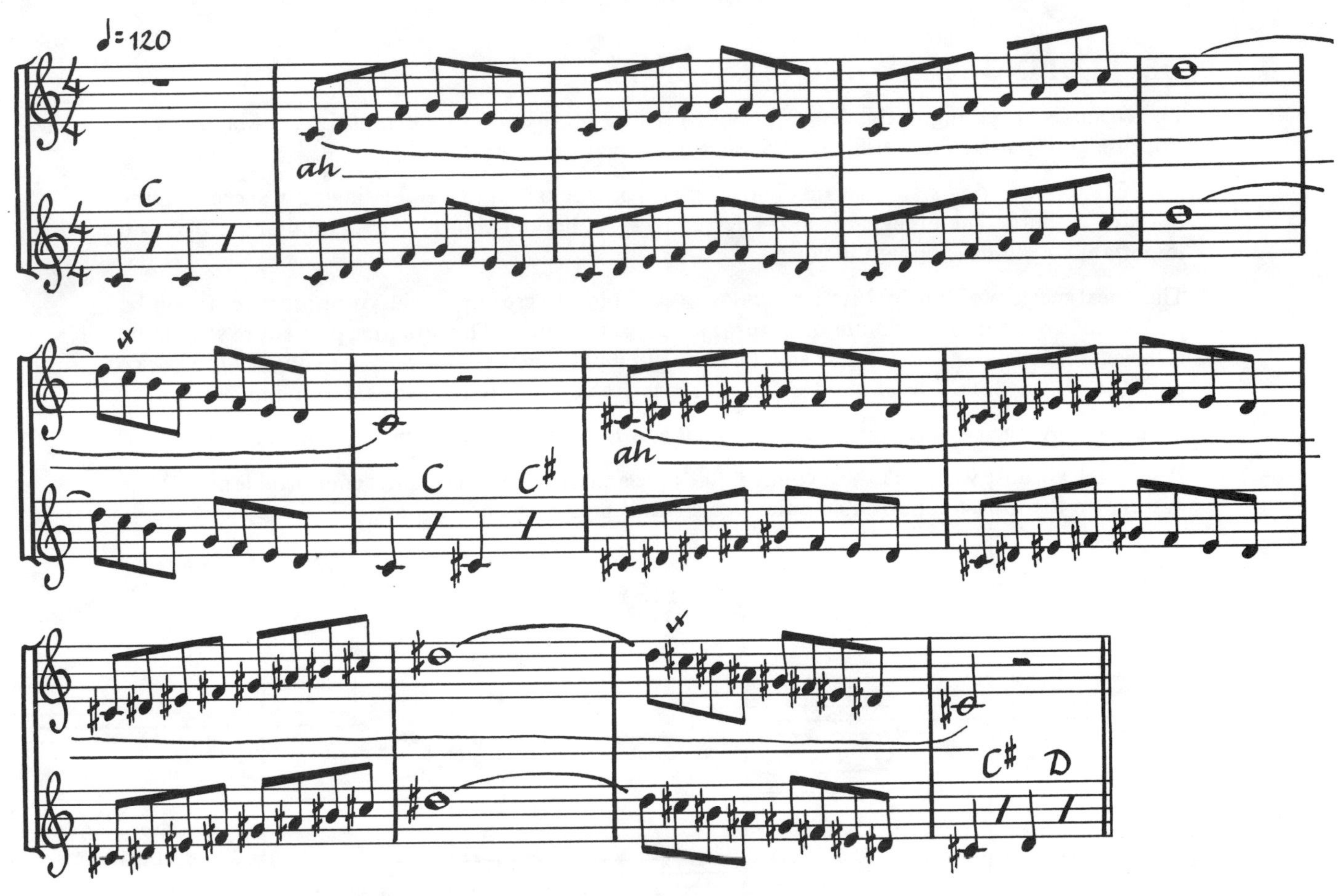

VOCALISE (9-3)

DEVELOPING THE VOICE—LESSON TEN

The vocalises appearing in this lesson provide practice on the notes that comprise the Major chord. Vocalise (10-3) also includes the Major scale up to the fifth degree.

ARPEGGIO *(are-PEJ-ee-oh)* means "harplike." An arpeggio is produced by singing in succession the notes of a chord. The arpeggio is also referred to as a "broken chord." Arpeggio practice plays an important role in developing the voice.

The vocal masters of the "old Italian school" were in total agreement that vocal practice should be performed softly in the medium or natural range of the voice. This practice procedure should be followed for several months. There should be no attempt to increase the range or volume of the voice until the student feels at ease and the vocal organs are completely relaxed when singing.

When singing, the conscious mind sets the goal and the subconscious mind accomplishes it.

Begin each vocalise with the lowest comfortable note and ascend to the highest comfortable note. Then descend to the lowest comfortable note. Use a sneak breath when necessary.

VOCALISE (10-1)

ascend by half-steps to highest comfortable note
descend by half-steps to lowest comfortable note

VOCALISE (10-2)

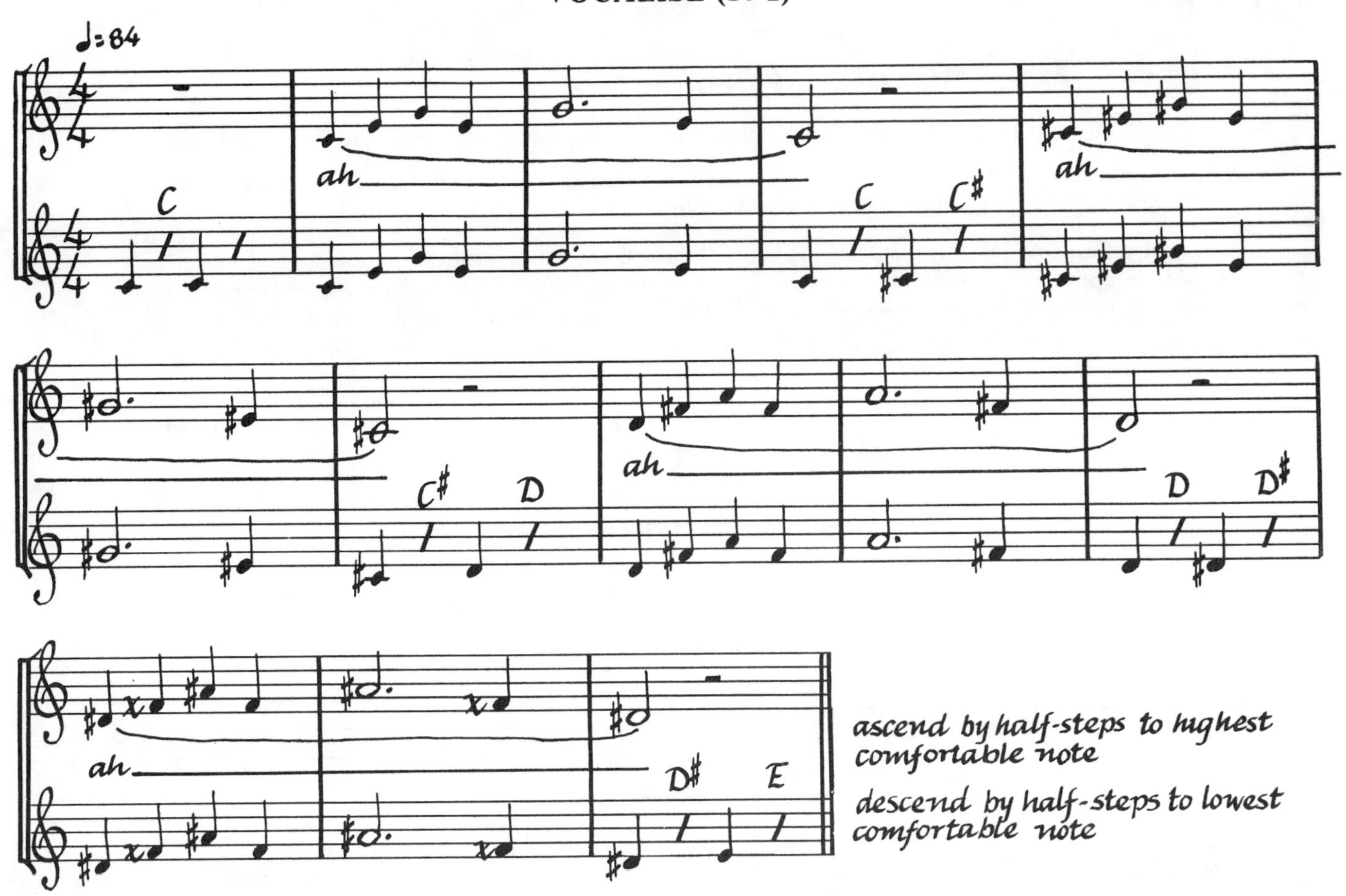

VOCALISE (10-3)

DEVELOPING THE VOICE—LESSON ELEVEN

The vocalises in Lesson Eleven afford arpeggio and scale practice up to an interval of an octave.

Vocal abuse is a common occupational hazard for athletic coaches, cheerleaders, teachers, ministers, factory workers, politicians and enthusiastic sports fans.

Loud yelling and loud strained singing cause the vocal cords to vibrate with greater force and over a wider amplitude than required for everyday communication. When the vocal cords and voice muscles are strained beyond their normal limits, the result can be hoarseness and mild laryngitis. This condition usually clears up after one-time abuse, but becomes a problem when the vocal cords are not given an opportunity to rest and bounce back to normal.

The physical sensations that accompany the production of low, medium, and high-pitched tones have led to the terms "chest register," "middle register," and "head register."

Begin each exercise with the lowest comfortable note and ascend to the highest comfortable note. Then descend to the lowest comfortable note. Use a catch breath when necessary.

VOCALISE (11-1)

VOCALISE (11-2)

ascend by half-steps to highest comfortable note
descend by half-steps to lowest comfortable note

VOCALISE (11-3)

DEVELOPING THE VOICE—LESSON TWELVE

This lesson provides arpeggio practice spanning an interval of an octave, and scale practice up to an interval of a ninth.

Continued vocal abuse caused by yelling or by loud strained singing can result in the formation of a nodule on the vocal cord. This occurs when the continued irritation of swollen vocal cords actually causes bleeding into the voice muscle tissue.

Vocal abuse also becomes a problem when there is an attempt to compensate for hoarseness or laryngitis by developing an improper way of producing the voice. This faulty voice production may continue even after the original hoarseness disappears.

The act of singing is so physiologically complex that it is well that nature has relegated the duty to the subconscious.

Begin each vocalise with the lowest comfortable note and ascend to the highest comfortable note. Then descend to the lowest comfortable note. Use a sneak breath when necessary.

VOCALISE (12-1)

ascend by half-steps to highest comfortable note
descend by half-steps to lowest comfortable note

VOCALISE (12-2)

ascend by half-steps to highest comfortable note
descend by half-steps to lowest comfortable note

VOCALISE (12-3)

ascend by half-steps to highest comfortable note
descend by half-steps to lowest comfortable note

DEVELOPING THE VOICE—LESSON THIRTEEN

This lesson provides practice in the staccato *(stac-CAH-toe).* The word STACCATO is from the Italian and means "separated." A note with a dot either above or below is to be performed in a staccato manner. The time value of a note which is sung staccato is cut short (abbreviated by approximately one-half). Despite the abbreviation of a note that is performed staccato, the full time value must elapse before the next note is sung.

The four vocalises that follow contain the staccato and are important for developing the voice. Do not take a breath for each note that is sung staccato. Instead, sing each series of staccato notes on one breath.

Begin each vocalise with the lowest comfortable note and ascend to the highest comfortable note. Then descend to the lowest comfortable note.

VOCALISE (13-1)

ascend by half-steps to highest comfortable note
descend by half-steps to lowest comfortable note

VOCALISE (13-2)

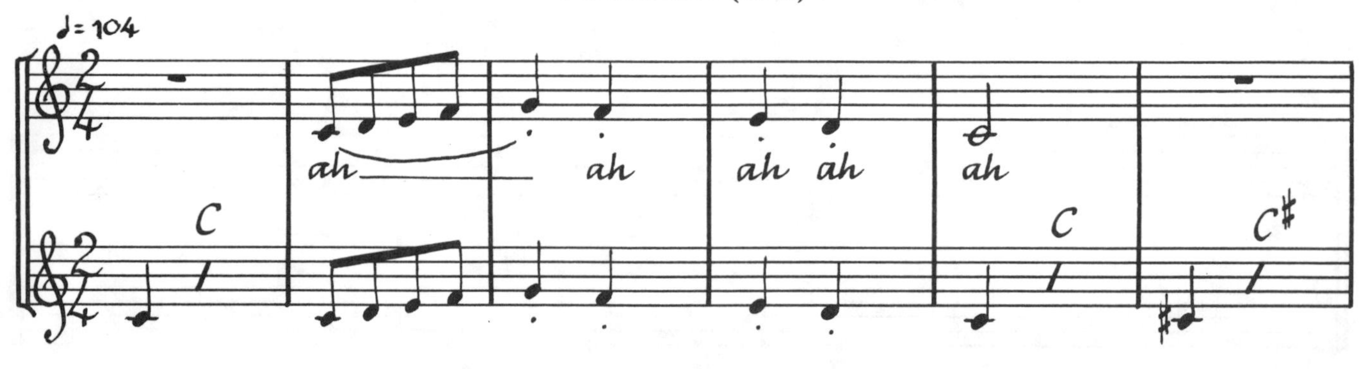

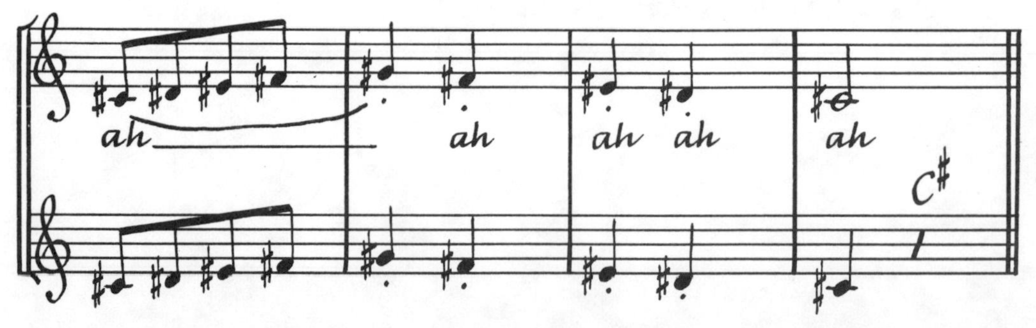

ascend by half-steps to highest comfortable note
descend by half-steps to lowest comfortable note

VOCALISE (13-3)

♩=104
ah
ah ah ah
ah
C
C C♯
ah
ah ah ah
ah
C♯ D
ah
ah ah ah
ah
D D♯
ascend by half-steps to highest comfortable note
descend by half-steps to lowest comfortable note
VOCALISE (13-4)
♩=104
ah
ah ah ah
ah ah
ah
ah
C
C
C♯
ah ah ah
ah ah
ah
ah
ah ah ah
C♯
D
ah ah ah
ah
D
D♯
ascend by half-steps to highest comfortable note
descend by half-steps to lowest comfortable note

DEVELOPING THE VOICE—LESSON FOURTEEN

This lesson provides practice in scalewise studies and in singing intervals of an octave.

The production of a vocal tone is one of nature's greatest wonders. The singer has merely to think of the pitch he would like to produce and then, by some mysterious means, the vocal cords quickly and subconsciously adjust to the required tension. The breath is then expelled and the imagined pitch is produced. This is the equivalent of a violinist turning the pegs of his instrument without sounding the strings, then starting to play and finding the strings perfectly tuned.

On the day of a performance the warmup and light vocalises are to be practiced. Failure to limber up the voice before a singing engagement places a strain on the vocal cords and could mar the performance. Also, too much practice prior to an engagement is equally harmful.

Begin each exercise with the lowest comfortable note and ascend to the highest comfortable note. Then descend to the lowest comfortable note. Use a sneak breath when necessary.

VOCALISE (14-1)

ascend by half-steps to highest comfortable note
descend by half-steps to lowest comfortable note

VOCALISE (14-2)

ascend by half-steps to highest comfortable note
descend by half-steps to lowest comfortable note

VOCALISE (14-3)

ascend by half-steps to highest comfortable note
descend by half-steps to lowest comfortable note

SOLMIZATION *(sole-muh-ZAY-shun)*—French spelling is *solmisation.*

Solmization refers to the use of the syllables, do, re, mi, fa, sol, la, and ti, to name the tones of the scale when singing vocal exercises, melodies and harmonies.

These syllables afford the student practice in singing the various vowel sounds.

All preceding vocal exercises have been limited to the syllable "AH." Because this syllable causes the throat to open wide, it is ideal for teaching the pupil the "feeling" of the open throat.

When practicing the solmization exercises that follow, the student will attempt to maintain the same open throat position for all the syllables as though they were the syllable "AH."

PRONUNCIATION OF THE SOLMIZATION SYLLABLES

The syllable Do is pronounced *dough.*
The syllable Re is pronounced *ray.*
The syllable Mi is pronounced *mee.*
The syllable Fa is pronounced *fah.*
The syllable Sol is pronounced *so.*
The syllable La is pronounced *lah.*
The syllable Ti is pronounced *tee.*

FUTURE PRACTICE PERIODS

Unlike the study of a musical instrument where the pupil begins with the most rudimentary exercises and advances with each succeeding lesson to studies that become increasingly complex, the student of voice continues to practice the same lessons which were studied at the very beginning. This is because with the study of voice the first vocalises are as important as the more advanced studies.

The student is to practice each solmization lesson for one week, starting with Solmization (15-1), (15-2), (15-3) in Lesson Fifteen. In addition, on the first day, vocalise Lesson One is to be practiced. On the second day vocalise Lesson Two is to be practiced. On the third day vocalise Lesson Three is to be practiced, etc.

On the following week in Lesson Sixteen, during which Solmization (16-1), (16-2), (16-3) are practiced, vocalises eight through fourteen are to be practiced, so that a different vocalise is studied each day of the week.

Each succeeding week a new solmization lesson is to be practiced, while at the same time a different vocalise is practiced each day. On the day following completion of the fourteen vocalises, the pupil is to return to vocalise one and begin over again.

The vocalises are important to insure that the open throat position is maintained and that the delivery is completely relaxed. The solmizations provide the pupil with practice on the various vowel sounds, and offer preparation for the study of sight singing.

Begin each solmization exercise with the lowest comfortable note and ascend to the highest comfortable note. Then descend to the lowest comfortable note. Breathe wherever it is comfortable and in good musical taste. The solmization studies are to be sung legato.

Note: Cassette tape #RL 6943 is available to demonstrate and provide accompaniment for the solmizations that follow.

DEVELOPING THE VOICE—LESSON FIFTEEN

DEVELOPING THE VOICE—LESSON SIXTEEN
SOLMIZATION (16-1)
♩= 104
do re mi fa
fa mi re do
do re mi fa
mi re do
C
C♯
ascend by half-steps to highest comfortable note
descend by half-steps to lowest comfortable note
SOLMIZATION (16-2)
♩= 104
do re mi
re mi fa
mi fa mi fa
mi re do
C
C♯
ascend by half-steps to highest comfortable note
descend by half-steps to lowest comfortable note
SOLMIZATION (16-3)
♩= 104
do mi fa mi
fa mi re
do
C
C♯
D
ascend by half-steps to highest comfortable note
descend by half-steps to lowest comfortable note

DEVELOPING THE VOICE—LESSON SEVENTEEN

DEVELOPING THE VOICE—LESSON EIGHTEEN

SOLMIZATION (18-1)

SOLMIZATION (18-2)

SOLMIZATION (18-3)

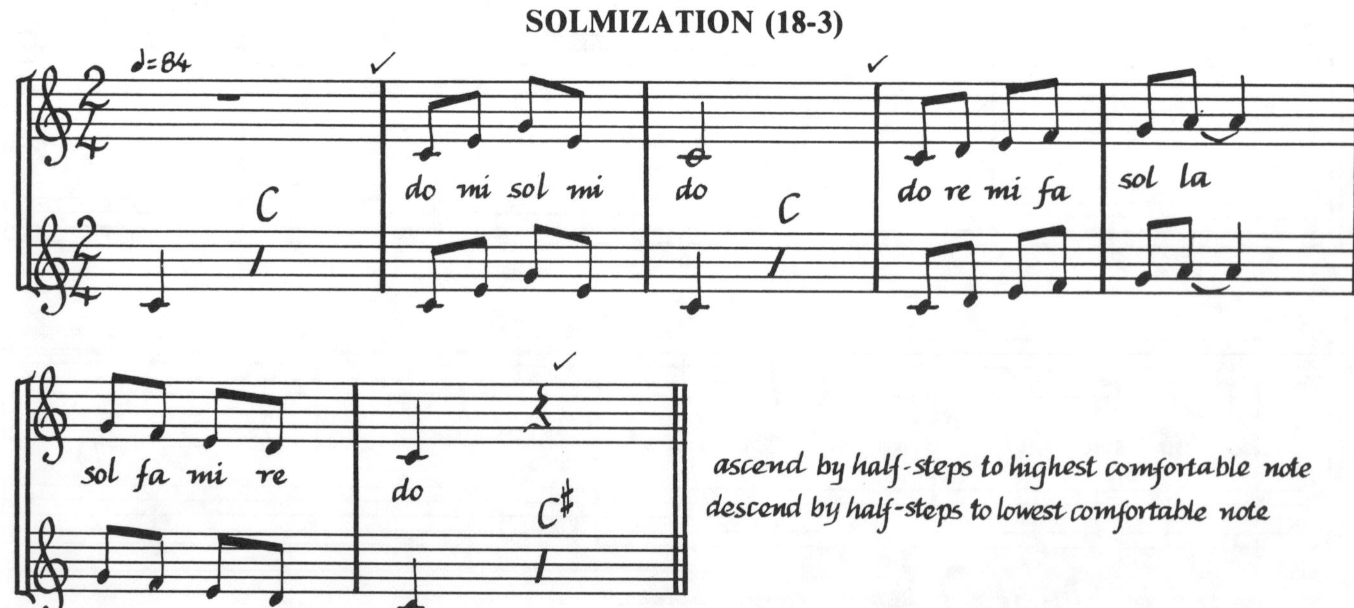

DEVELOPING THE VOICE—LESSON NINETEEN

SOLMIZATION (19-3)

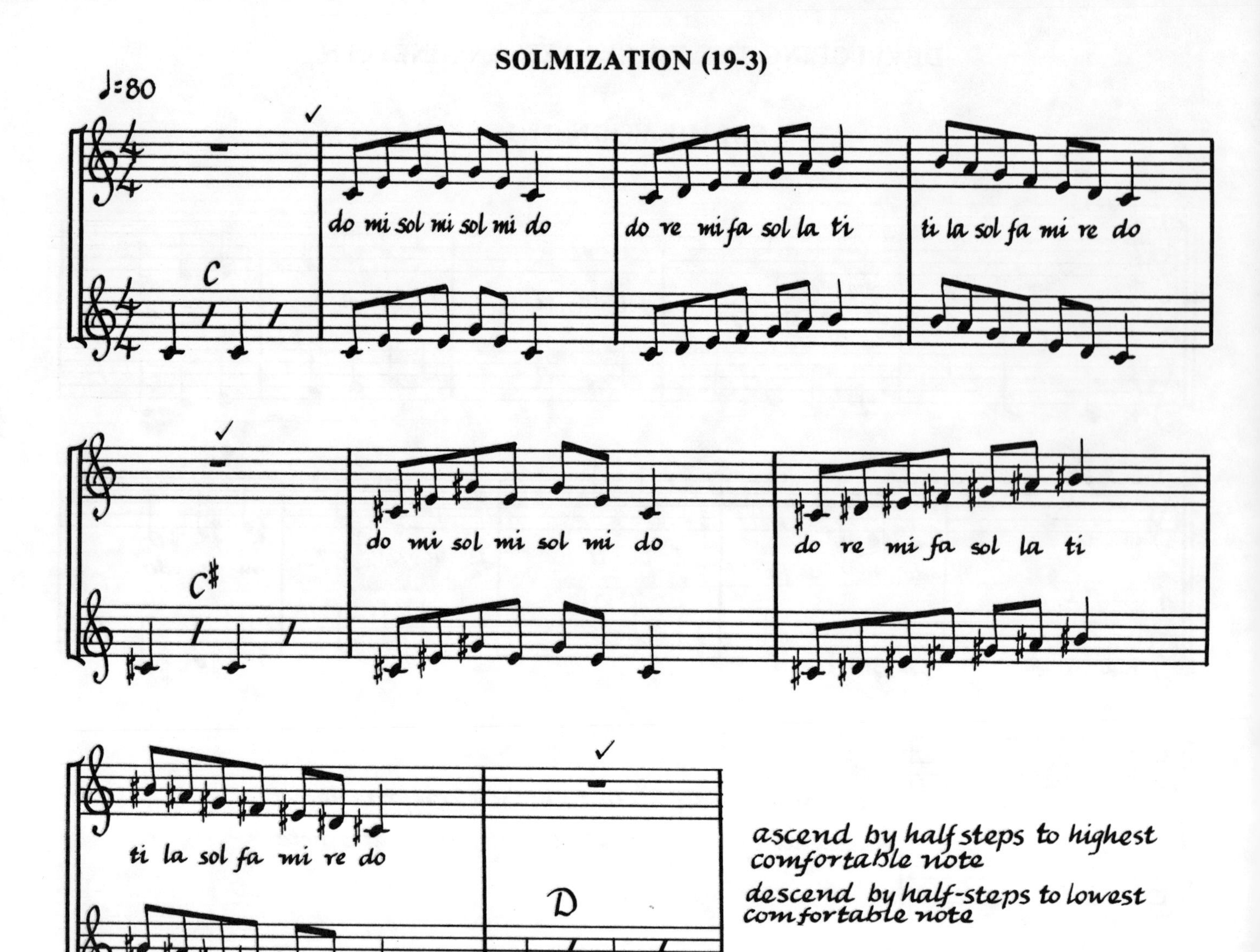

SOLMIZATION (20-1)

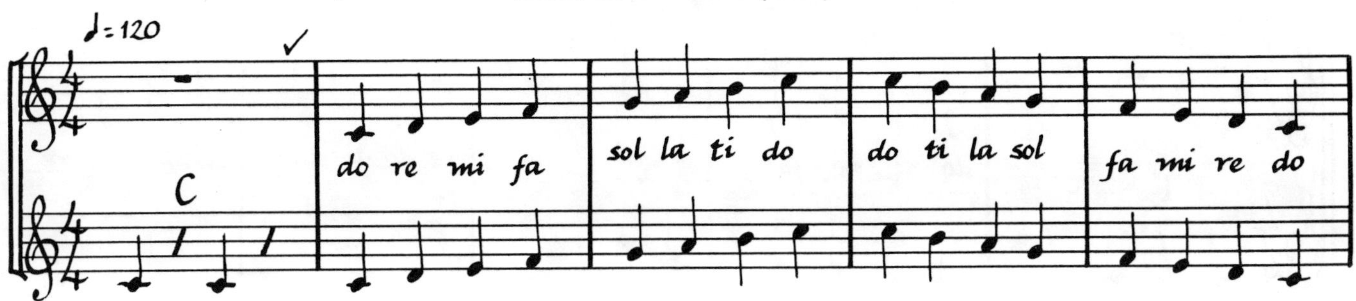

ascend by half-steps to highest comfortable note
descend by half-steps to lowest comfortable note

SOLMIZATION (20-2)

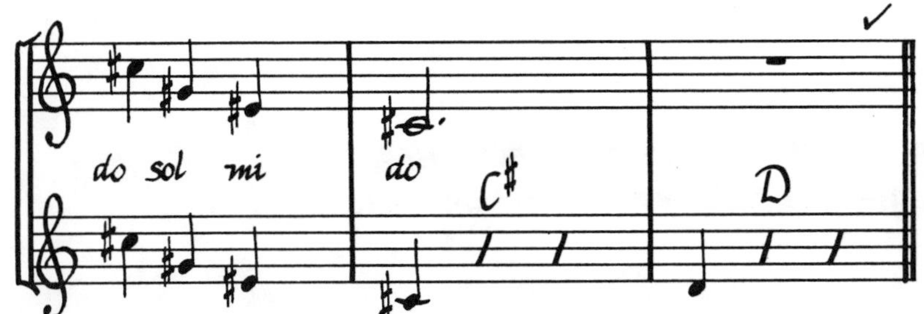

ascend by half-steps to highest comfortable note
descend by half-steps to lowest comfortable note

SOLMIZATION (20-3)

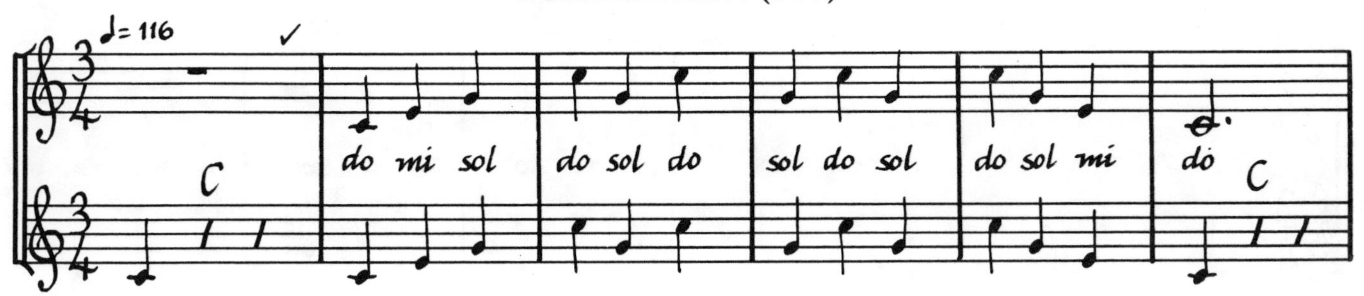

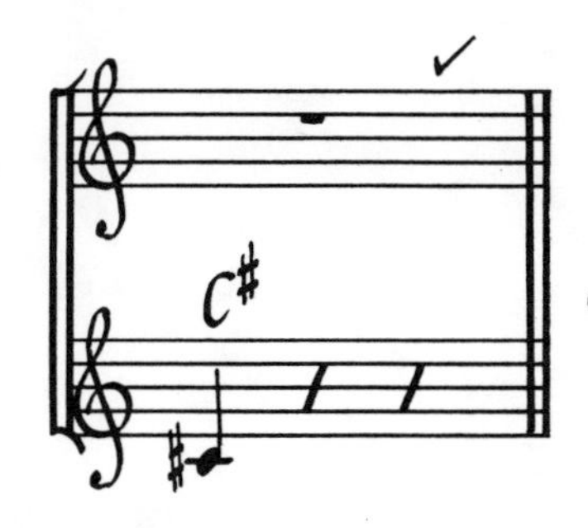

ascend by half-steps to highest comfortable note
descend by half-steps to lowest comfortable note

DEVELOPING THE VOICE—LESSON TWENTY-ONE

SOLMIZATION (21-1)

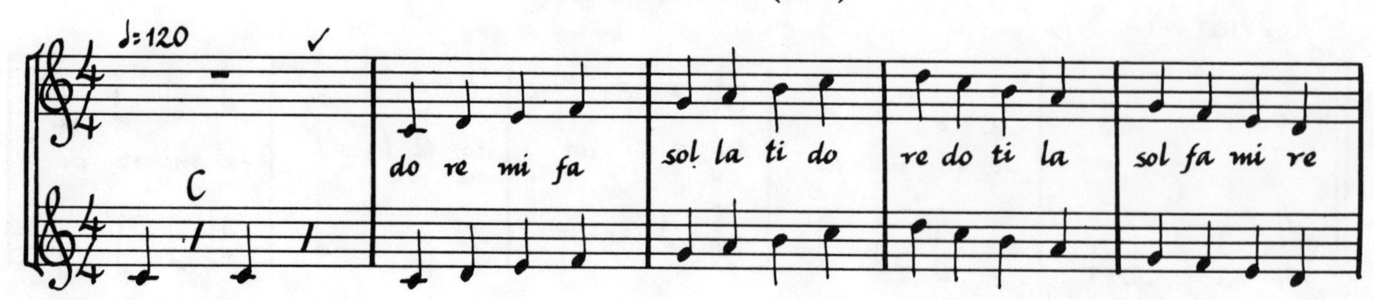

ascend by half-steps to highest comfortable note
descend by half-steps to lowest comfortable note

SOLMIZATION (21-2)

ascend by half-steps to highest comfortable note
descend by half-steps to lowest comfortable note

SOLMIZATION (21-3)

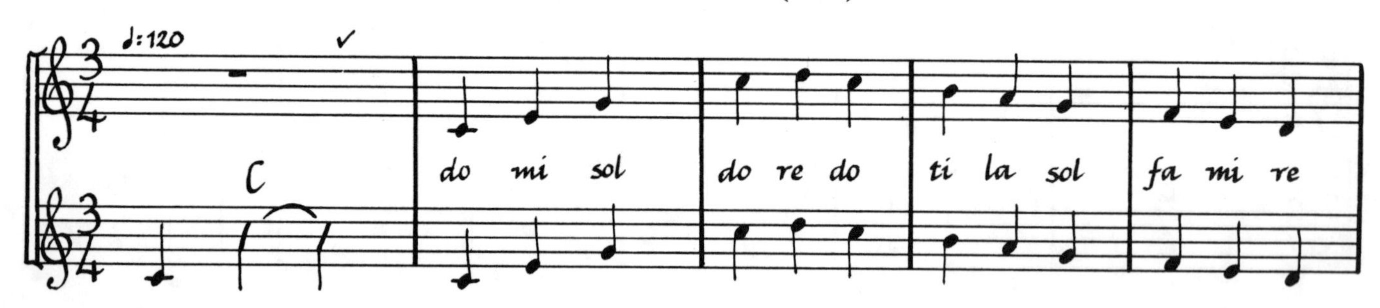

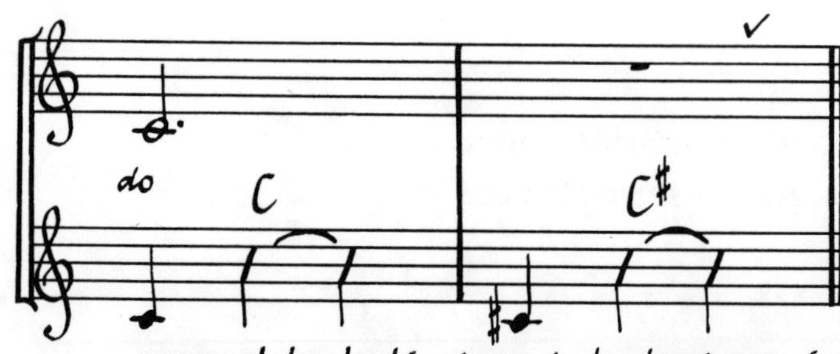

ascend by half-steps to highest comfortable note
descend by half-steps to lowest comfortable note

REGARDING SOLMIZATION

This completes the solmization studies appearing in this section. Proceed to Section Three which begins on page 96, for application of the solmization syllables to Ear Training and Sight Singing. At the same time, continue with Music Theory in Section Two.

REGARDING THE VOCALISES

Continued practice of the fourteen vocalises is essential for further development of the voice. A different vocalise is to be practiced each day. No harm will result if, on occasion, vocalise practice is missed for one or two days. At times it will be found that the voice improves after a respite of a few days.

REGARDING MUSIC THEORY

The study of Music Theory in Section Two is to be continued until the final theory lesson has been completed.

REGARDING DELIVERY TECHNIQUE AND SHAPING A SONG FOR PERFORMANCE

In addition to advancing to Section Three—Ear Training and Sight Singing—the pupil is to proceed to Section Four—Delivery Technique and Shaping a Song for Performance—which begins on page 135.

SECTION TWO

MUSIC THEORY

Music theory unlocks the door to the mysteries of music. It breaks down barriers between the singer and accompanist. It enables the vocal coach to suggest that a song be ended on the Major Seventh rather than the Tonic, knowing that the singer will comprehend his meaning.

Music theory frees the singer from searching for a musician to transpose the music that is too high or too low for the voice. It provides the knowledge to change a melodic line, which the singer finds uncomfortable, by substituting notes of the accompaniment chord.

Music theory enlightens the singer about how he may lower or raise melodic segments an octave so that a phrase is within his range. It allows the singer to intelligently discuss a vocal arrangement with the music director, conductor, orchestra leader, group leader, arranger, composer, recording engineer, coach, music teacher, accompanist, master of ceremonies, or sound mixer.

Just imagine if your family physician or your lawyer or accountant were suddenly unable to read English. Each of them could continue to function—with outside help, of course—but they would not be as efficient. The same is true of the singer who is unfamiliar with music theory. True, the singer can function, even on a professional level, but not with the effectiveness that a knowledge of music theory will provide.

The voice student who becomes proficient in music theory enjoys a decided advantage.

The vocal assignments appearing in this section are to help the student become familiar with music notation. They are not intended as vocal exercises, and are to be sung very softly and without the slightest strain.

MUSIC THEORY—LESSON ONE

THE STAFF

Printed music is written on five horizontal lines and the spaces between them.

The five lines and four spaces are called THE STAFF.

The lines and spaces of the staff are numbered from the bottom upward.

5th line
4th line — 4th space
3rd line — 3rd space
2nd line — 2nd space
1st line — 1st space

In addition to their number names, the lines and spaces possess letter names.

Reading upward, the lines are named E G B D F. This may be remembered by thinking of the sentence: Every Good Boy Deserves Fun.

The spaces are named F A C E, which may be remembered by thinking of the word "FACE," which rhymes with "space."

F — E — D — C — B — A — G — F — E

THE NOTE o

To represent pitch (highness or lowness of tone) and time duration of a musical sound, a sign called a NOTE is employed.

A low-pitched tone is represented by a note on the lower portion of the staff. A tone which is high in pitch is represented by a note on the upper portion of the staff.

When a note is too low or else too high to be accommodated within the confines of the staff, the note is placed below or else above the staff.

THE LETTER NAME OF A NOTE IS THE SAME AS THAT OF THE LINE OR SPACE IT OCCUPIES ON THE STAFF.

THE "F" NOTE THE "E" NOTE THE "B" NOTE

THE MUSICAL ALPHABET CONSISTS OF SEVEN LETTERS: A B C D E F G

The staff may be considered a musical stairway ascending and descending alphabetically in a sequence of line, space, line, space, etc.

Reading from the bottom upward, the first line is "E." The first space is "F." The second line is "G." The second space is "A." The third line is "B." The third space is "C," and so forth.

The space below the first line is "D." The space above the fifth line is "G." The first line below the staff is "C."

THE TREBLE CLEF SIGN

By enclosing the 2nd line "G" with its scroll, the TREBLE CLEF SIGN establishes the location of the note "G" on the staff. Because the lines and spaces of the staff are named alphabetically, knowing where the "G" note appears serves as a bearing from which the names of all lines and spaces can be determined. The treble clef sign is also called the G CLEF SIGN. The staff upon which the treble clef sign appears is called the TREBLE STAFF. In popular sheet music, the vocal part is written on the treble staff.

ASSIGNMENT: Using letter names, the student is to name each of the notes appearing below. This is to be done at least three successive times each day.

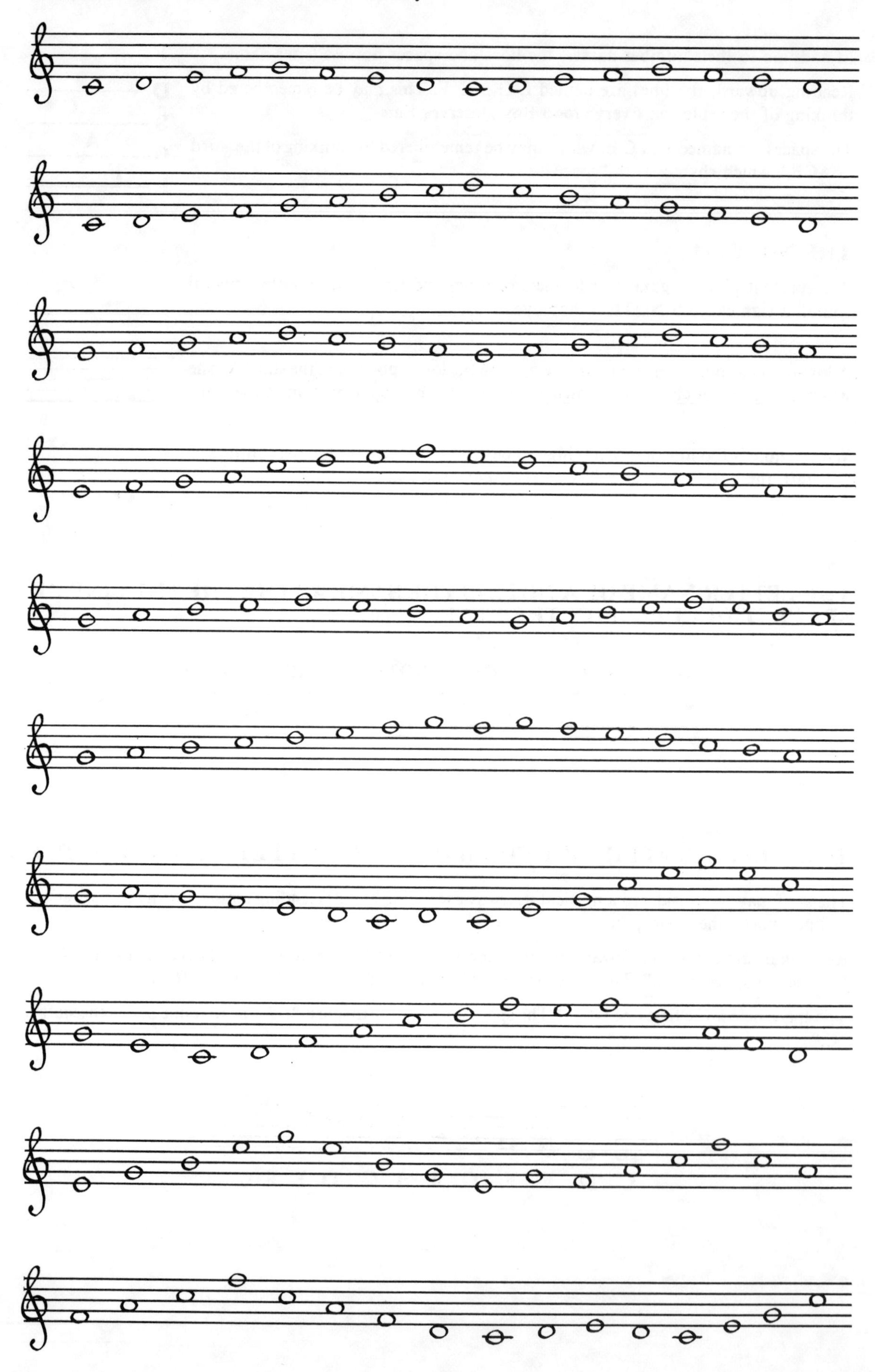

MUSICAL TIME

To perform music properly, the singer must not only sing the correct notes, but must sustain the notes for the proper duration of time.

Unlike clock time which is measured in seconds, minutes and hours, musical time is measured by a system of BEATS. One beat of musical time is represented by a down and up motion of the foot (down beat and up beat).

NOTES MAY BE WRITTEN IN MANY SHAPES

While the placement of a note on the staff indicates the letter name of the note, the shape of the note advises the performer of its TIME VALUE (number of beats for which the note is sustained).

THE QUARTER NOTE

The quarter note is comprised of two parts, a HEAD and a STEM. The stem of the quarter note may point either up or down, depending upon the location of the note head on the staff.

When the note head appears below the middle line of the staff, the stem will point in an upward direction. When the note head appears above the middle line of the staff, the stem will point in a downward direction. When the note head appears on the middle line of the staff, the stem may point either up or down, though in engraved music the stem usually points downward.

THE QUARTER NOTE RECEIVES ONE BEAT

The time value of the quarter note is 1 BEAT. This means that the quarter note is sustained for the time required to complete one beat of the foot (down beat and up beat).

1 BEAT

THE QUARTER REST

A REST is an interval of silence. The time value of the quarter rest is 1 BEAT. When a quarter rest occurs, silence prevails for the time required to complete one beat of the foot (down beat plus up beat).

1 BEAT OF SILENCE

In the music below, melody notes are shown as quarter notes with stems pointing upward. Foot beats are shown as quarter notes with stems pointing downward.

Each beat consists of both the down beat (downward motion) and the up beat (upward motion) of the foot. The foot is to beat time at a steady, even rate.

ASSIGNMENT ONE: While slowly beating time with the foot, sing the music below. Do not sing the words. Instead sing the syllable "LA." When singing an unfamiliar melody and the Rhythm Exercise, sing "LA" on one pitch throughout. During those beats on which a quarter rest occurs, there is to be vocal silence.

This music theory assignment is to be performed once each day. This lesson is not intended as a vocal exercise; it serves to familiarize the student with the reading of musical time. It is to be sung softly and without the slightest trace of strain.

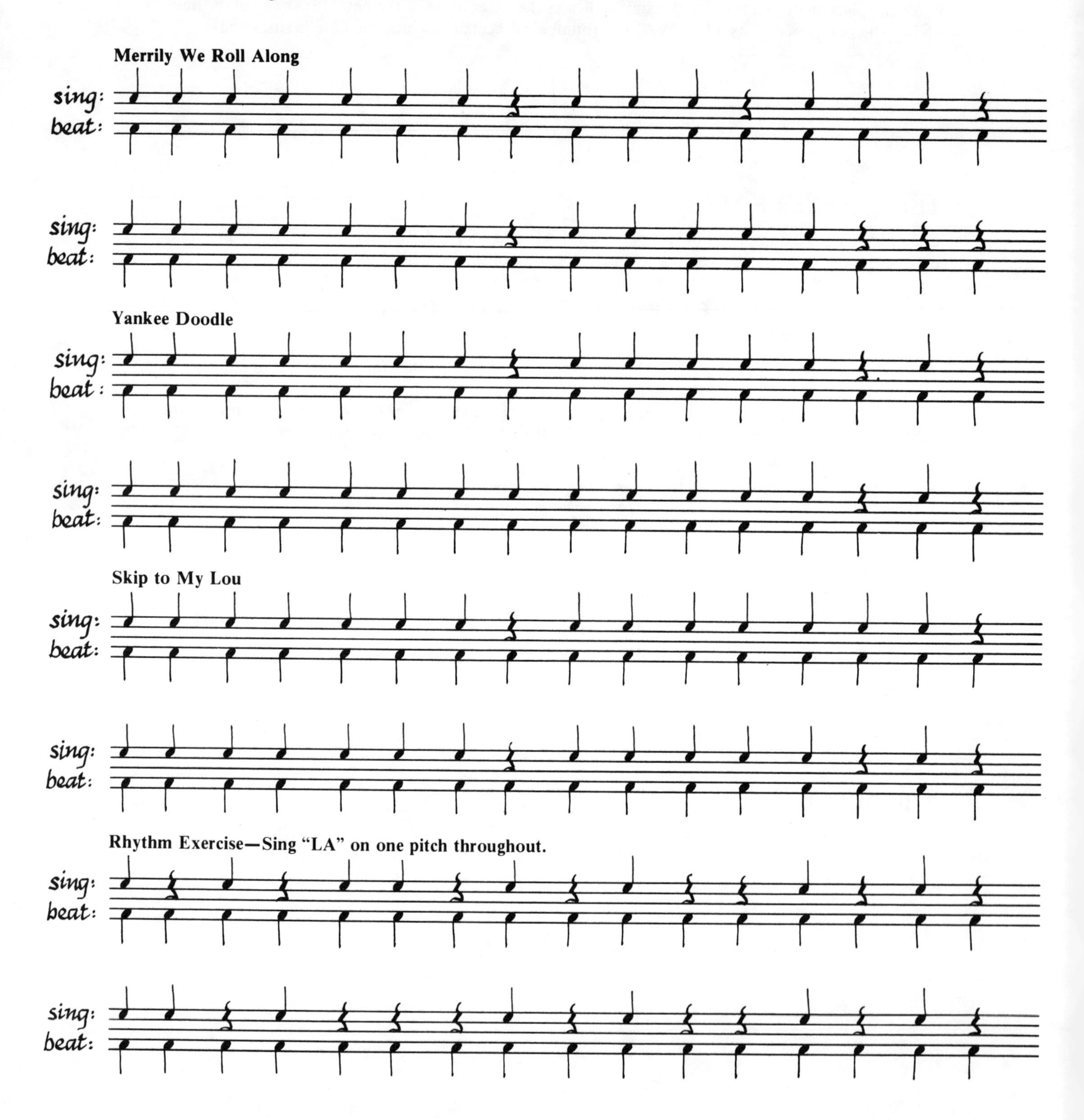

ASSIGNMENT TWO: Using letter names, the student is to name each of the notes appearing below. This is to be done at least two successive times each day.

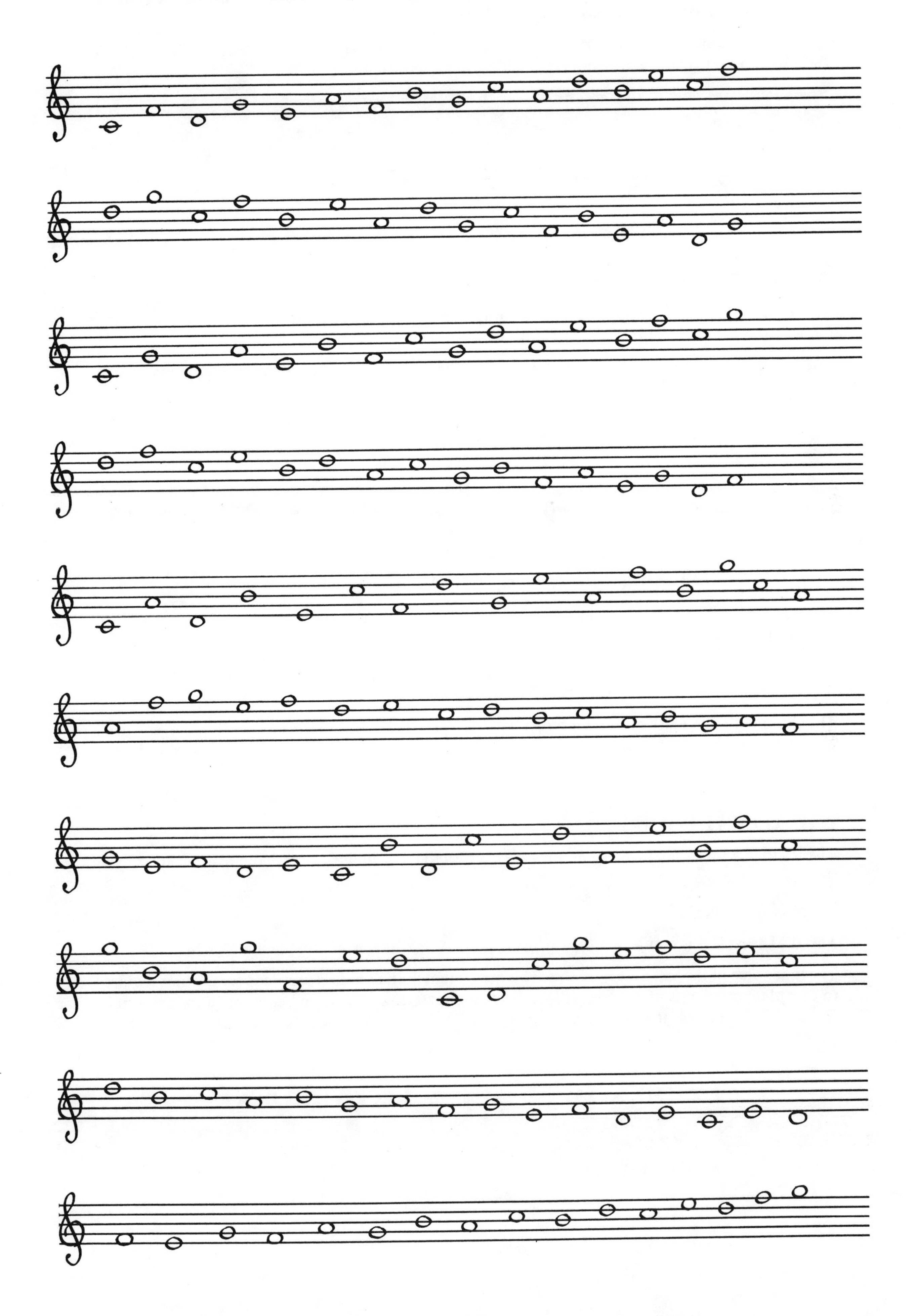

MUSIC THEORY—LESSON THREE

BAR LINES AND MEASURES

The staff is divided into sections called MEASURES. The vertical lines which divide the staff into measures are called either BARS or BAR LINES.

To indicate the end of a section or strain of music, a double bar is used. A double bar consisting of one light bar and one heavy bar denotes the end of a composition.

Some musicians refer to the "measure" as a "bar." Either term is correct.

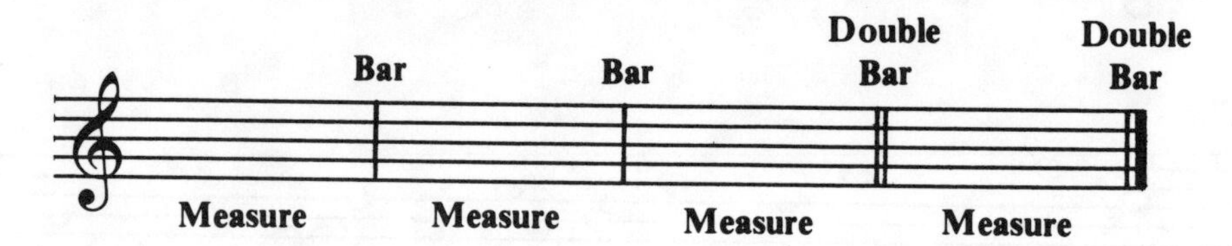

THE TIME SIGNATURE

The TIME SIGNATURE consists of two numbers, one above the other, which offer the player information concerning the music that follows.

The numerator (upper number) indicates the number of beats occurring within each measure. The denominator (lower number) indicates the note type that receives one beat.

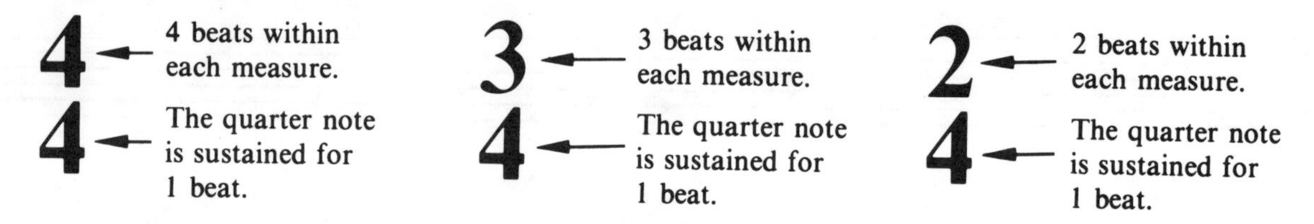

The TIME SIGNATURE appears at the beginning of a composition, to the right of the clef sign.

COMMON TIME C

4/4 time occurs so frequently and is so common to all types of music that it is called COMMON TIME. Another means of expressing Common Time is by the sign C.

The Common Time sign does not represent the letter "C." Its origin stems from the Middle Ages when a circle was used by the church musicians to represent music written in 3/4 time, and a broken circle to represent 4/4 time. The present-day Common Time sign is an embellished version of the broken circle.

THE REPEAT SIGN :||

The REPEAT SIGN instructs the performer to return to the beginning of the composition and to play the music once again.

THE HALF NOTE 𝅗𝅥

The HALF NOTE is comprised of two parts, a HEAD, which is hollow, and a STEM.

The time value of the half note is 2 beats. This means that the half note is sustained for the time required to complete two beats of the foot (down beat, up beat, down beat, up beat). As in the arithmetic fractions 1/2 and 1/4, the half note is equal to twice the time value of the quarter note.

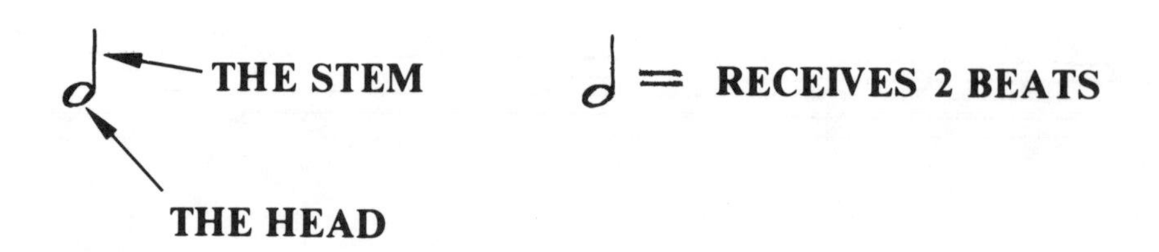

ASSIGNMENT ONE: At least two successive times each day, name each of the notes appearing below.

ASSIGNMENT TWO: At least twice each day, sing the following melodies while beating time. Do not sing the words. Instead sing the syllable "LA" for the quarter notes and half notes. Tones which are sung for one beat (quarter note) are to be sustained throughout the down beat and the up beat. Tones sung for two beats (half note) are to be sustained throughout the down beat, up beat, down beat, up beat. If the melody is unfamiliar, sing "LA" on one pitch throughout. Begin singing the melody with any tone that feels comfortable. Sing softly and without the slightest trace of strain.

MUSIC THEORY—LESSON FOUR

THE DOTTED HALF NOTE

The time value of a dot is one half the value of the note appearing to its left. Since the half note receives two beats, the value of the dot is one beat. Therefore, the dotted half note is sustained for a total of three beats (down beat, up beat, down beat, up beat, down beat, up beat).

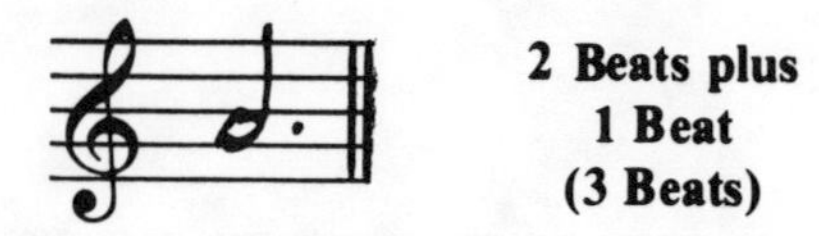

2 Beats plus
1 Beat
(3 Beats)

ASSIGNMENT ONE: At least two successive times each day, name each of the notes appearing below.

ASSIGNMENT TWO: At least twice each day, sing the following melodies while beating time. Do not sing the words. Instead sing the syllable "LA" for each of the notes. If the melody is unfamiliar, sing "LA" on one pitch throughout. Begin singing the melody with any tone that feels comfortable. Sing softly and without the slightest trace of strain.

MUSIC THEORY—LESSON FIVE

THE TIE

The tie is a curved line joining two notes of the same pitch. Time values of tied notes are added. Therefore, when two notes are tied, the first note is sung and is sustained for the total time value of the two notes.

3 BEATS **5 BEATS**

ASSIGNMENT ONE: At least two successive times each day, name each of the notes appearing below.

ASSIGNMENT TWO: At least twice each day, sing the following melody while beating time. Do not sing the words. Instead sing the syllable "LA" for each of the notes. If the melody is unfamiliar, sing "LA" on one pitch throughout. Begin singing the melody with any tone that feels comfortable. Sing softly and without the slightest trace of strain.

The Sidewalks of New York

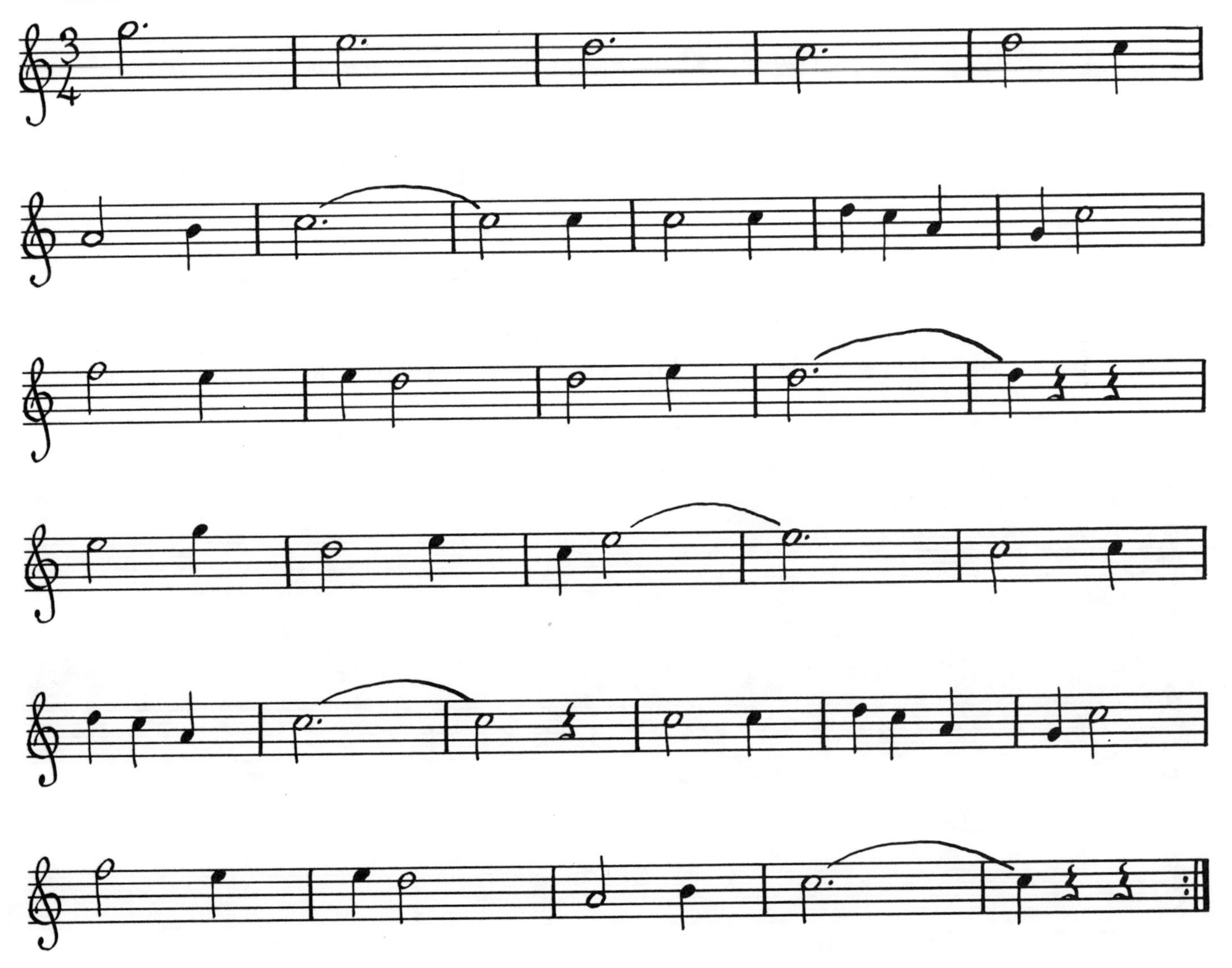

MUSIC THEORY—LESSON SIX

THE HALF REST represents an interval of silence for two beats. 

LEGER LINES

At times a musical composition contains notes that are too high or else too low to be accommodated by the staff. For example, a note that is higher than "G" (1 space above the 5th line) or lower than "D" (1 space below the 1st line). When this occurs it is necessary to add short lines above or below the staff upon which notes may be placed on or between. These added lines are called LEGER LINES (sometimes spelled "ledger lines").

The student is to become familiar with the following notes.

THE WHOLE NOTE

The WHOLE NOTE is comprised of a head, which is hollow. It has no stem.

THE WHOLE NOTE RECEIVES FOUR BEATS

The whole note is sustained for four beats (down beat, up beat, down beat, up beat, down beat, up beat, down beat, up beat).

4 beats

ASSIGNMENT ONE: At least two successive times each day, name each of the notes appearing in the following melodies.

ASSIGNMENT TWO: At least twice each day, sing the following melodies while beating time. Do not sing the words. Instead sing the syllable "LA" for each of the notes. If the melody is unfamiliar, sing "LA" on one pitch throughout. Begin singing the melody with any note that feels comfortable. Sing softly and without the slightest trace of strain.

PICK-UP NOTES

Notes appearing before the first complete measure, that do not comprise the total time value required to produce a full measure, are called PICK-UP NOTES. When pick-up notes occur, those beats that are lacking for the completion of the measure are found at the end of the selection. Thus, the first and the final measures, each incomplete in itself, add up to one full measure.

Marines Hymn

MUSIC THEORY—LESSON SEVEN

THE "G" NOTE

NOTES WE HAVE LEARNED

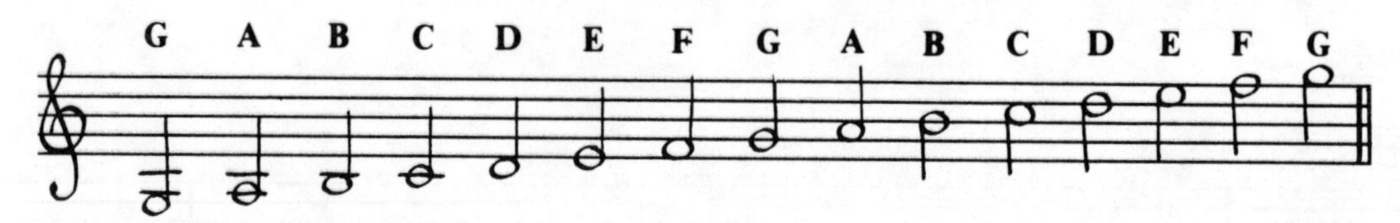

ASSIGNMENT ONE: At least two successive times each day, name each of the notes appearing in the following melody.

ASSIGNMENT TWO: At least twice each day, sing the following melody while beating time. Do not sing the words. Instead sing the syllable "LA" for each of the notes. If the melody is unfamiliar, sing "LA" on one pitch throughout. Begin singing the melody with any pitch that feels comfortable. Sing softly and without the slightest trace of strain.

Grandfather's Clock

MUSIC THEORY—LESSON EIGHT

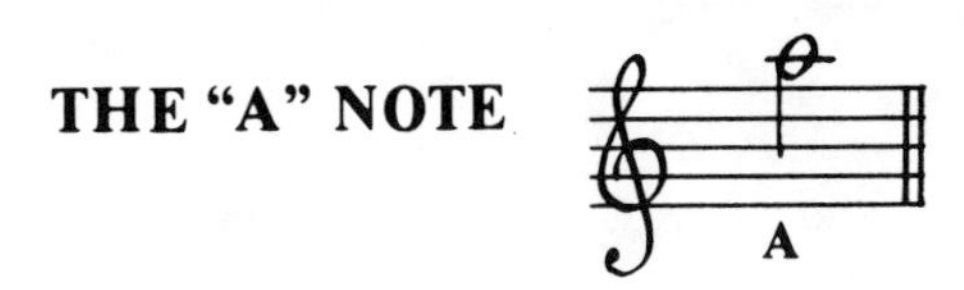

NOTES WE HAVE LEARNED

ASSIGNMENT ONE: At least two successive times each day, name each of the notes appearing in the following melody.

ASSIGNMENT TWO: At least twice each day, sing the following melody while beating time. Do not sing the words. Instead sing the syllable "LA" for each of the notes. If the melody is unfamiliar, sing "LA" on one pitch throughout. Begin singing with any tone that feels comfortable. Sing softly and without the slightest trace of strain.

MUSIC THEORY—LESSON NINE

THE EIGHTH NOTE

The EIGHTH NOTE is comprised of three parts. A head, a stem and a flag. The flag always appears to the right of the stem.

When two or more consecutive eighth notes occur, the flags may be omitted and the notes joined together by a BEAM. The choice of the flag or beam is determined by whether the music is written for instrument or voice.

When music is written for "voice" (vocal music), the eighth notes are usually written with flags. This is to facilitate the placement of the notes above the word syllables to be sung.

In instrumental music, eighth notes are usually written with a beam.

When vocal music does not include lyrics, eighth notes may be written with either beams or flags.

THE EIGHTH NOTE RECEIVES ONE HALF BEAT

The time value of the eighth note is 1/2 BEAT. This means that the eighth note is sustained for the time required to complete either the down beat of the foot or the up beat. Two consecutive eighth notes comprise one beat—one note on the down beat and one note on the up beat.

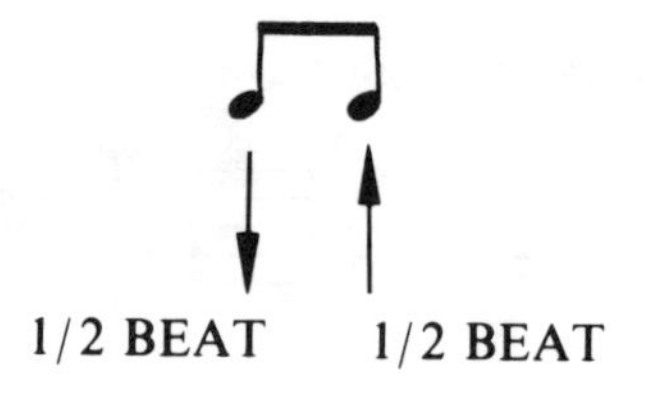

COUNTING TIME FOR EIGHTH NOTES

Until this point all the notes we have learned were begun on the DOWN BEAT. Because the eighth note may begin on the UP BEAT as well as the DOWN BEAT, our manner of counting must now accommodate those notes which begin on the UP BEAT.

Whenever eighth notes appear, the "beat number" is counted on the down beat, and the word "and" is counted on the up beat.

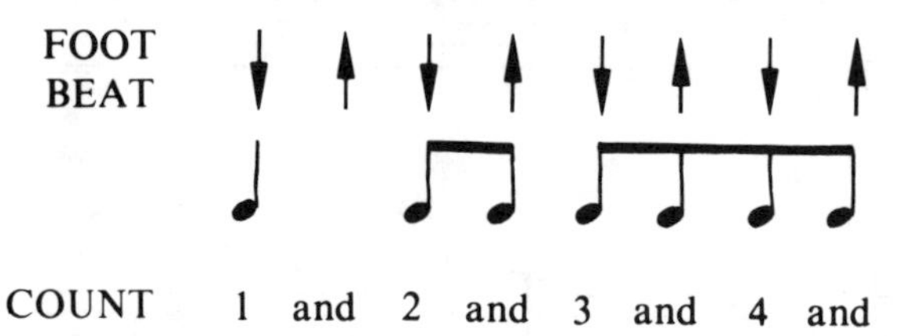

THE EIGHTH REST

The time value of the eighth rest is 1/2 BEAT. When an eighth rest occurs, silence prevails for the time required to complete either the down beat or the up beat of the foot, depending upon which part of the beat the rest appears.

THE WHOLE REST

The WHOLE REST represents an interval of silence for four beats. In addition, the WHOLE REST represents a whole measure rest. For example, in 3/4 time a whole rest represents 3 beats of silence.

Notice that the whole rest hangs down from the 4th line of the staff, whereas the half rest, which is similar in appearance, rises from the 3rd line of the staff.

To easily identify the whole rest, the student may find it helpful to think of the whole rest being of greater value (than the half rest), and therefore heavier, so that it hangs down from the 4th line of the staff. The half rest, being of lesser value, and therefore lighter, will rise from the 3rd line of the staff.

ASSIGNMENT ONE: At least two successive times each day, name each of the notes appearing in the following melodies.

ASSIGNMENT TWO: At least twice each day, sing the following melodies while beating time. Do not sing the words. Instead sing the syllable "LA" for each of the notes. If the melody is unfamiliar, sing "LA" on one pitch throughout. Begin singing the melody with any note that feels comfortable. Sing softly without the slightest trace of strain.

MUSIC THEORY—LESSON TEN

THE DOTTED QUARTER NOTE

The time value of a dot is one half the value of the note appearing to its left. Since the quarter note receives one beat, the value of the dot is one half beat. Therefore, the dotted quarter note is sustained for a total of one and one half beats (down beat, up beat, down beat).

THE DOTTED QUARTER NOTE FOLLOWED BY THE EIGHTH NOTE

A common rhythm pattern is that of the dotted quarter note followed by the eighth note.

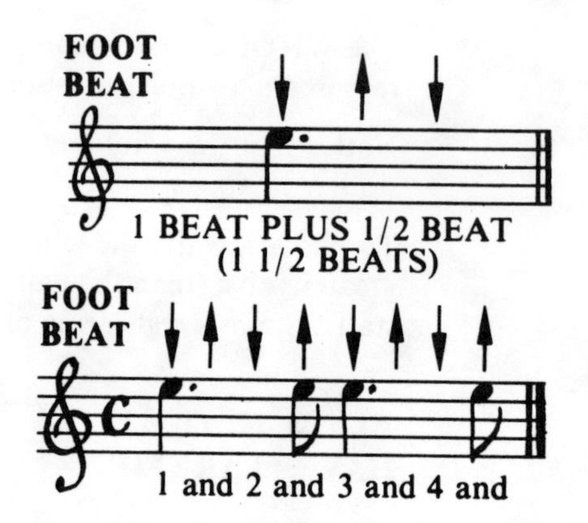

ASSIGNMENT ONE: At least two successive times each day, name each of the notes appearing in the following melodies.

ASSIGNMENT TWO: At least twice each day, sing the following melodies while beating time. Do not sing the words. Instead sing the syllable "LA" for each of the notes. If the melody is unfamiliar, sing "LA" on one pitch throughout. Begin singing the melody with any pitch that feels comfortable. Sing softly without the slightest trace of strain.

WHOLE STEPS AND HALF STEPS

On all musical instruments and the human voice, the notes "B" and "C," and also the notes "E" and "F," are closer to each other than any other two adjacent notes we have learned. The musician refers to the skip from "B" to "C," and from "E" to "F," as a half step (sometimes called a "half tone"). The separation of the other adjacent notes is one step (sometimes called "one tone" or a "whole tone").

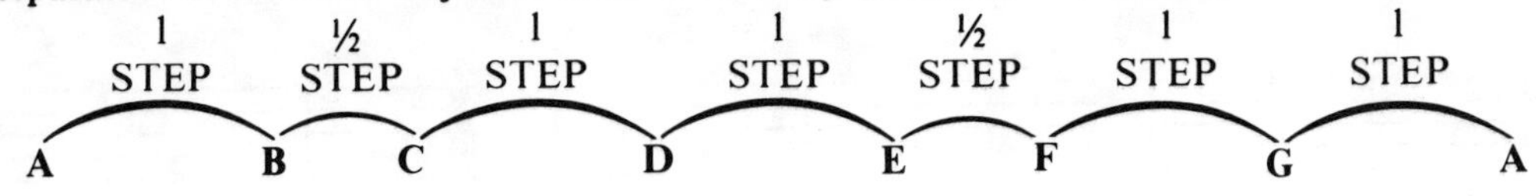

THE SHARP ♯

The **SHARP** is a musical sign that appears to the left of the note it governs. ♯♩

The sharped note is one half step higher than the natural (unsharped) note.

"A" sharp is one half step higher than "A"; "C" sharp is one half step higher than "C," etc. One half step higher than "B" is "C"; one half step higher than "E" is "F." If "B" sharp should appear in the music, "C" is to be performed. If "E" sharp appears, "F" is to be performed.

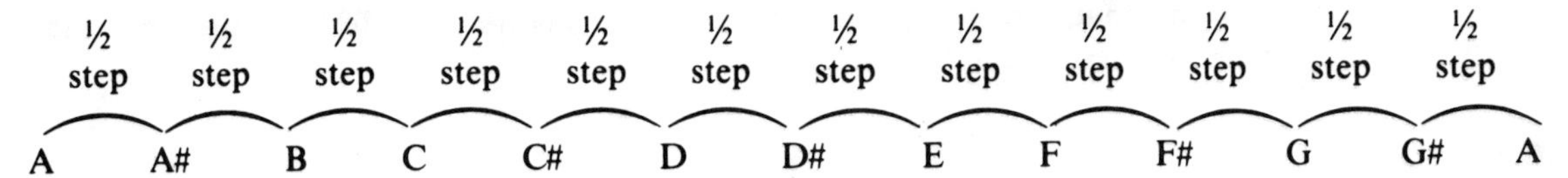

ASSIGNMENT ONE: At least two successive times each day, name each of the notes appearing in the following melody.

ASSIGNMENT TWO: At least twice each day, sing the following melody while beating time. Do not sing the words. Instead sing the syllable "LA" for each of the notes. If the melody is unfamiliar, sing "LA" on one pitch throughout. Begin singing the melody with any note that feels comfortable. Sing softly and without the slightest trace of strain.

THE SHARP REMAINS IN EFFECT UNTIL CANCELLED BY THE BAR LINE

In addition to its effect upon the note it precedes, the sharp automatically applies to all notes of the same pitch that follow it within the same measure. If, for example, the note "F" is sharped, then all "F" notes following within the same measure (appearing on the same line or space) are also sharped. At the completion of the measure, at the bar line, the sharp is no longer in effect.

ASSIGNMENT ONE: At least two successive times each day, name each of the notes appearing in the following melody.

ASSIGNMENT TWO: At least twice each day, sing the following melody while beating time. Do not sing the words. Instead sing the syllable "LA" for each of the notes. If the melody is unfamiliar, sing "LA" on one pitch throughout. Begin singing the melody with any note that feels comfortable. Sing softly and without the slightest trace of strain.

AN EXCEPTION TO THE RULE

The sharp is cancelled by the bar line EXCEPT in the case of a tie. When a sharped note is tied to a note occurring in the following measure, the tied note is also sharped.

EXAMPLE 1

The last note of the first measure and the first note of the second measure ("A" note) are both sharped. The last note of the second measure ("A" note) is NOT sharped.

EXAMPLE 2

The second and fourth notes of the first measure and the first note of the second measure ("C" note) are sharped. The third note of the second measure ("C" note) is NOT sharped.

ASSIGNMENT ONE: At least two successive times each day, name each of the notes appearing in the following melody and the EXERCISE IN SHARPS AND NATURALS.

ASSIGNMENT TWO: At least twice each day, sing the following melody while beating time. Do not sing the words. Instead sing the syllable "LA" for each of the notes. If the melody is unfamiliar, sing "LA" on one pitch throughout. You may begin singing the melody with any tone that feels comfortable. Sing softly and without the slightest trace of strain.

THE NATURAL SIGN ♮

The NATURAL is a musical sign that appears to the left of the note which it governs.

The NATURAL cancels the sharp. When a measure contains a sharped note which is followed by a "normal" note of the same letter, the natural sign precedes the normal note to inform the player that the note is not sharped.

In the example to the right, "C" sharp is followed by "C" natural.

THE FLAT ♭

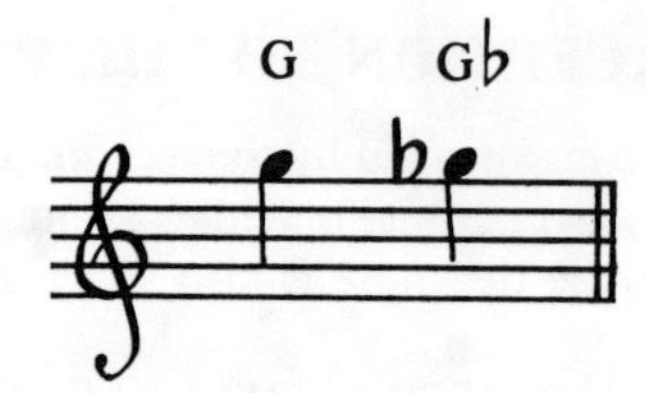

The **FLAT** is a musical sign that appears to the left of the note which it governs.

A FLATTED NOTE is one half step lower than the natural note.

ENHARMONICS

THE NOTES F# AND Gb ARE ENHARMONICS.

When two words sound alike but have different meanings (such as "pale" and "pail"), they are called "homonyms." When two musical notes sound alike but have different names, they are called "ENHARMONICS." For example, "F sharp" and "G flat" are enharmonics. "F sharp" is the enharmonic of "G flat." "G flat" is the enharmonic of "F sharp."

Enharmonics occur between all natural notes with the exception of B and C, and E and F.

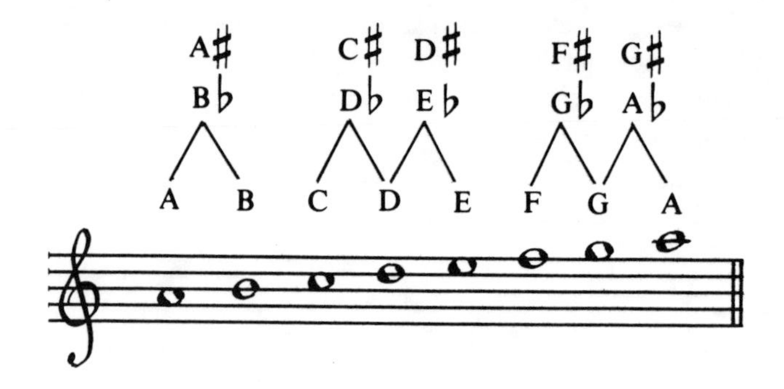

A SHORT QUIZ

What is the enharmonic of G#? ____________

What is the enharmonic of F#? ____________

What is the enharmonic of C#? ____________

What is the enharmonic of A#? ____________

What is the enharmonic of D#? ____________

What is the enharmonic of Db? ____________

What is the enharmonic of Bb? ____________

What is the enharmonic of Eb? ____________

What is the enharmonic of Ab? ____________

What is the enharmonic of Gb? ____________

SHARPS AND FLATS ARE GOVERNED BY THE SAME RULES

THE FLAT REMAINS IN EFFECT UNTIL CANCELLED BY THE BAR LINE

In addition to its effect upon the note it precedes, the flat automatically applies to all notes of the same letter that follow it within the same measure. If, for example, the note "G" is flatted, then all "G" notes following within the same measure, appearing on the same line or space, are also flatted. At the completion of the measure, at the bar line, the flat is no longer in effect.

ALL FOUR NOTES ARE FLATTED.

ONLY THE FIRST NOTE IS FLATTED.

THE FIRST AND FOURTH NOTES ARE FLATTED.

THE TIE IS AN EXCEPTION TO THE RULE

The flat is cancelled by the bar line EXCEPT in the case of a tie. When a flatted note is tied to a note occurring in the following measure, the tied note is also flatted.

EXAMPLE 1

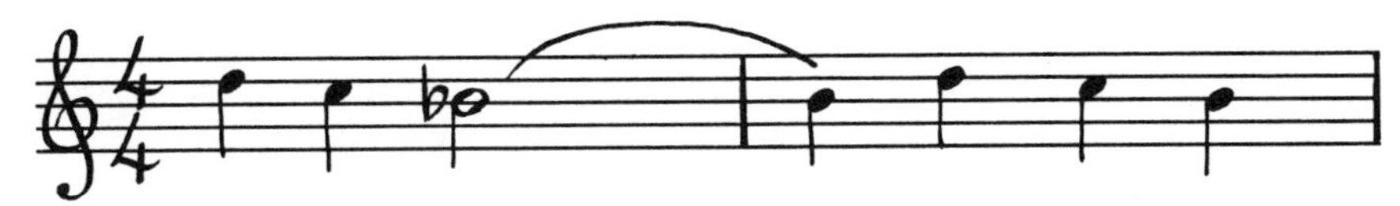

The last note of the first measure and the first note of the second measure ("B" note) are both flatted. The last note of the second measure ("B" note) is NOT flatted.

EXAMPLE 2

The second and fourth notes of the first measure and the first note of the second measure ("D" note) are flatted. The third note of the second measure ("D" note) is NOT flatted.

THE NATURAL ♮

The NATURAL is a musical sign that appears to the left of the note which it governs. ♮♩

The NATURAL cancels the flat.

THE DOUBLE SHARP 𝄪

The DOUBLE SHARP sign, when placed before a note, raises its pitch a whole step. The double sharp sign occurs rarely.

THE DOUBLE FLAT 𝄫

The DOUBLE FLAT sign, when placed before a note, lowers its pitch a whole step. The double flat sign occurs rarely.

A NEW SIGN

When a passage of music is to be repeated from a point other than the beginning of the selection, the following sign is placed at the point from which the music is to be repeated.

For example, music appearing between the double dotted bars is to be repeated.

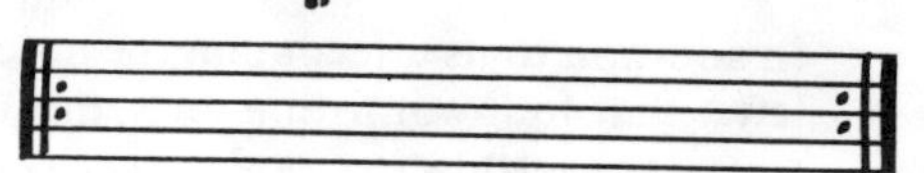

FIRST AND SECOND ENDINGS

To conserve space on the page and to avoid rewriting the same passage several times, the music writer frequently makes use of FIRST and SECOND ENDINGS.

When two endings occur, the singer will proceed until the repeat sign in the first ending. The music is then repeated as indicated. Upon repeating, the first ending is skipped, and the second ending is sung.

Although it is not usual, some selections have as many as three or four endings.

ASSIGNMENT ONE: At least two successive times each day, name each of the notes appearing in the following melody.

ASSIGNMENT TWO: At least twice each day, sing the following melody while beating time. Do not sing the words. Instead sing the syllable "LA" for each of the notes. If the melody is unfamiliar, sing "LA" on one pitch throughout. Begin singing the melody with any pitch that feels comfortable. Sing softly and without the slightest trace of strain.

MUSIC THEORY—LESSON FIFTEEN

TEMPO

In a musical selection or study, the speed or rapidity with which the beats follow each other is called the TEMPO. Some students erroneously consider whole notes to be "slow notes" and eighth notes to be "fast notes." Tempo is not determined by the appearance of whole notes or eighth notes within a composition, but rather by the pace of the pulse of the music.

WHAT ARE CHROMATIC SIGNS?

Sharps, flats, and naturals are called CHROMATICS. A CHROMATIC SIGN is therefore a sharp sign, a flat sign or a natural sign.

COURTESY CHROMATICS

Though the rules regarding chromatic signs are clear, there are times when the musician may feel unsure of the correct performance of certain segments of music. To provide clarification, the COURTESY CHROMATIC is used. The courtesy chromatic is not really necessary (as the term implies), but it serves as a reminder. Courtesy chromatics are sometimes enclosed in parentheses.

EXAMPLE:

ASSIGNMENT ONE: At least two successive times each day, name each of the notes appearing in the following melody.

ASSIGNMENT TWO: At least twice each day, sing the following melody while beating time. Do not sing the words. Instead sing the syllable "LA" for each of the notes. If the melody is unfamiliar, sing "LA" on one pitch throughout. Begin singing the melody with any tone that feels comfortable. Sing softly and without the slightest trace of strain.

Fascination

MUSIC THEORY—LESSON SIXTEEN

THE SIXTEENTH NOTE

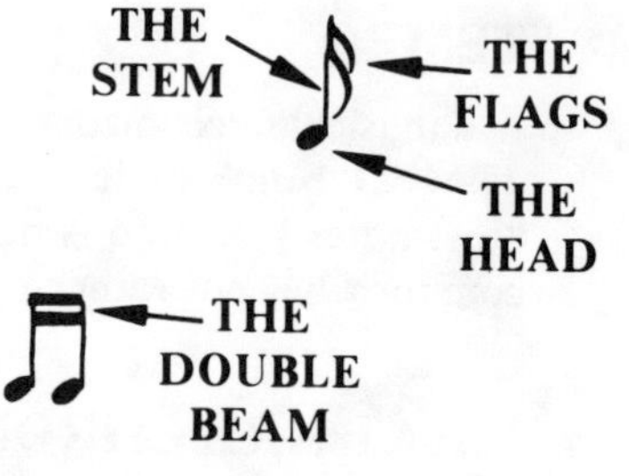

The SIXTEENTH NOTE is comprised of four parts: a head, a stem and two flags. The flags always appear to the right of the stem.

When two or more consecutive sixteenth notes occur, the flags may be omitted and the notes joined together by a DOUBLE BEAM. The choice of flags or beams is determined by whether the music is written for instrument or voice.

When music is written for "voice" (vocal music), the sixteenth notes are usually written with flags. This is to facilitate the placement of the notes above the syllables to be sung.

In instrumental music, sixteenth notes are usually written with beams.

When vocal music does not include lyrics, sixteenth notes may be written with either beams or flags.

THE SIXTEENTH NOTE RECEIVES ONE QUARTER BEAT

The time value of the sixteenth note is 1/4 BEAT. This means that the sixteenth note is sustained for the time required to complete the first or second half of the down beat, or the first or second half of the up beat of the foot. Four consecutive sixteenth notes comprise one beat—two notes on the down beat and two notes on the up beat.

THE SIXTEENTH REST

The time value of the sixteenth rest is 1/4 BEAT. Silence prevails for the time required to complete that portion of the beat on which the sixteenth rest occurs.

THE DOTTED EIGHTH NOTE

The time value of the dot is one half the value of the note appearing to its left. Since the eighth note receives 1/2 BEAT, the value of the dot is 1/4 BEAT. Therefore, the dotted eighth note is sustained for a total of three quarters of one beat (down beat and one half of the up beat).

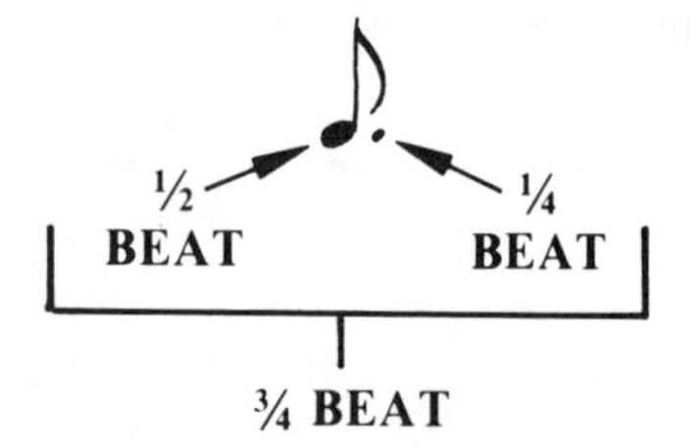

THE DOTTED EIGHTH NOTE FOLLOWED BY THE SIXTEENTH NOTE

The dotted eighth note followed by the sixteenth note is a common rhythm pattern.

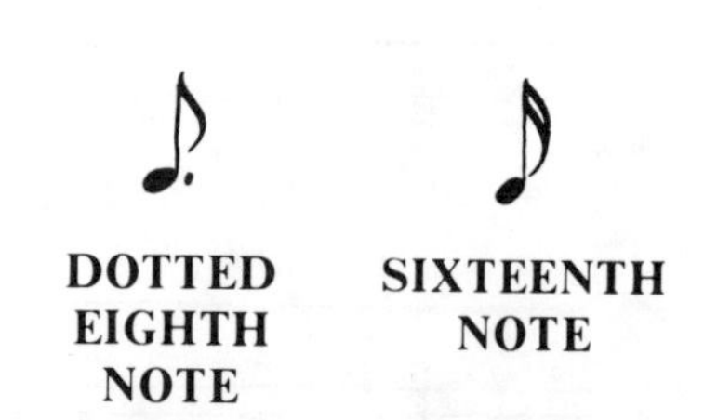

The dotted eighth note receives 3/4 of a beat. The sixteenth note receives 1/4 of a beat. Together, the dotted eighth note and the sixteenth note receive a total of one beat.

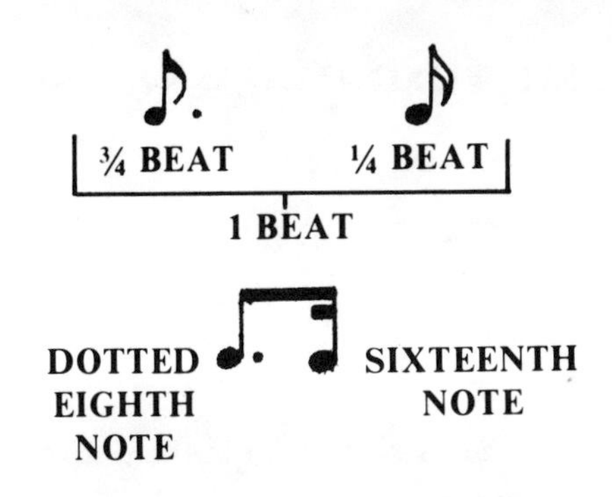

In instrumental music, when the dotted eighth note is followed by the sixteenth note, the dotted eighth note appears with a single beam. The sixteenth note is shown with the single beam and an additional short beam.

To count time for the dotted eighth note followed by the sixteenth note, the singer will sing the dotted eighth note during the "beat number" (1st beat, 2nd beat, 3rd beat, 4th beat) and the word "and." The sixteenth note is sustained for the time required to say "a."

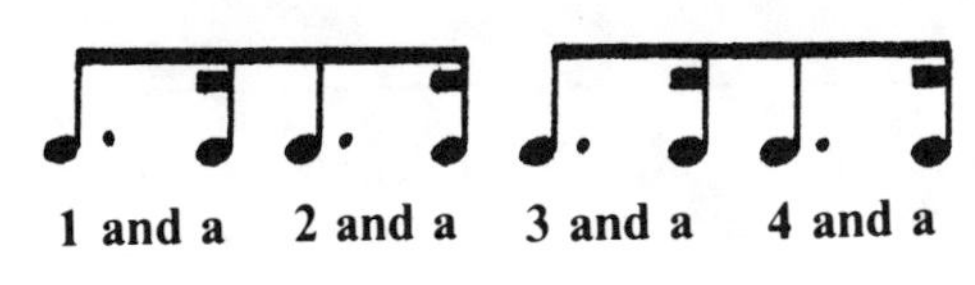

The performance of these two notes is similar to that of two eighth notes, except that the first eighth note is sustained slightly, and the second eighth note is abbreviated.

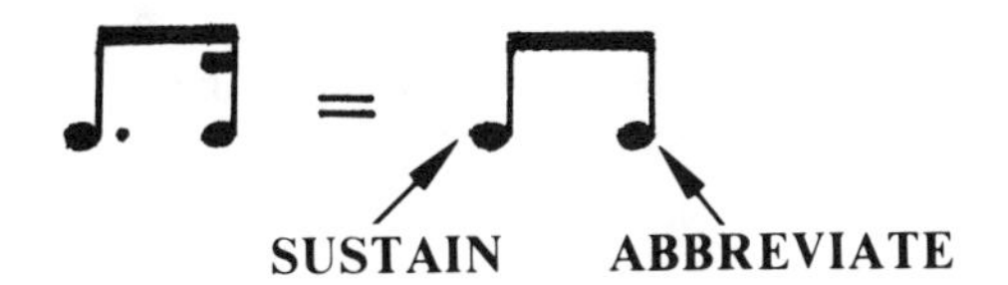

ASSIGNMENT ONE: At least two successive times each day, name each of the notes appearing in the following melody. Observe the repeat sign.

ASSIGNMENT TWO: At least twice each day, sing the following melody while beating time. Do not sing the words. Instead sing the syllable "LA" for each of the notes. If the melody is unfamiliar, sing "LA" on one pitch throughout. Begin singing the melody with any note that feels comfortable. Sing softly and without the slightest trace of strain.

MUSIC THEORY—LESSON SEVENTEEN

THE EIGHTH NOTE TRIPLET

The EIGHTH NOTE TRIPLET consists of three eighth notes with the number "3" placed above or below the center note.

A TRIPLET is performed in the time ordinarily given to two of the three notes.

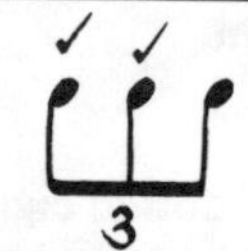

Because two eighth notes receive a total of one beat, the three notes comprising the triplet are sung within one beat.

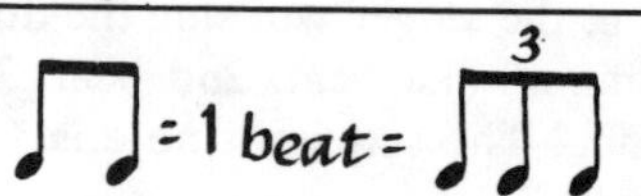

If a passage consists mainly or entirely of triplets, the number "3" may be omitted after the first measure. Immediately following is the word SIMILE, to indicate the continuation of the pattern. If the word SIMILE is omitted, the singer, by counting the beats within the measure, can determine whether a three-note grouping is an eighth note triplet or merely three eighth notes.

HOW TO PERFORM THE EIGHTH NOTE TRIPLET

To perform the eighth note triplet, one beat of the foot (down beat plus up beat) is divided into three equal parts.

The first note is sung as the foot executes the down beat. The second note is sung while the foot remains at rest upon the floor. The third note is sung during the up beat of the foot.

Before attempting to perform the eighth note triplet, the student can acquire the "feel" of the triplet pattern by beating the foot while saying a three-syllable word such as MER-RI-LY. The first syllable is spoken during the down beat. The second syllable is spoken while the foot is at rest upon the floor. The third syllable is spoken during the up beat of the foot.

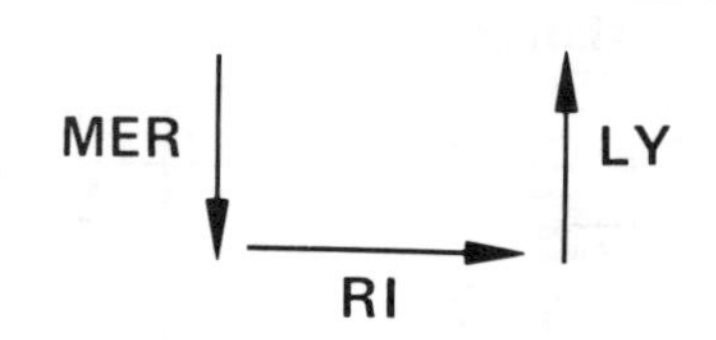

ASSIGNMENT ONE: At least two successive times each day, name each of the notes appearing in the following melody.

ASSIGNMENT TWO: At least twice each day, sing the following melody while beating time. Do not sing the words. Instead sing the syllable "LA" for each of the notes. If the melody is unfamiliar, sing "LA" on one pitch throughout. Begin singing the melody with any note that feels comfortable. Sing softly and without the slightest trace of strain.

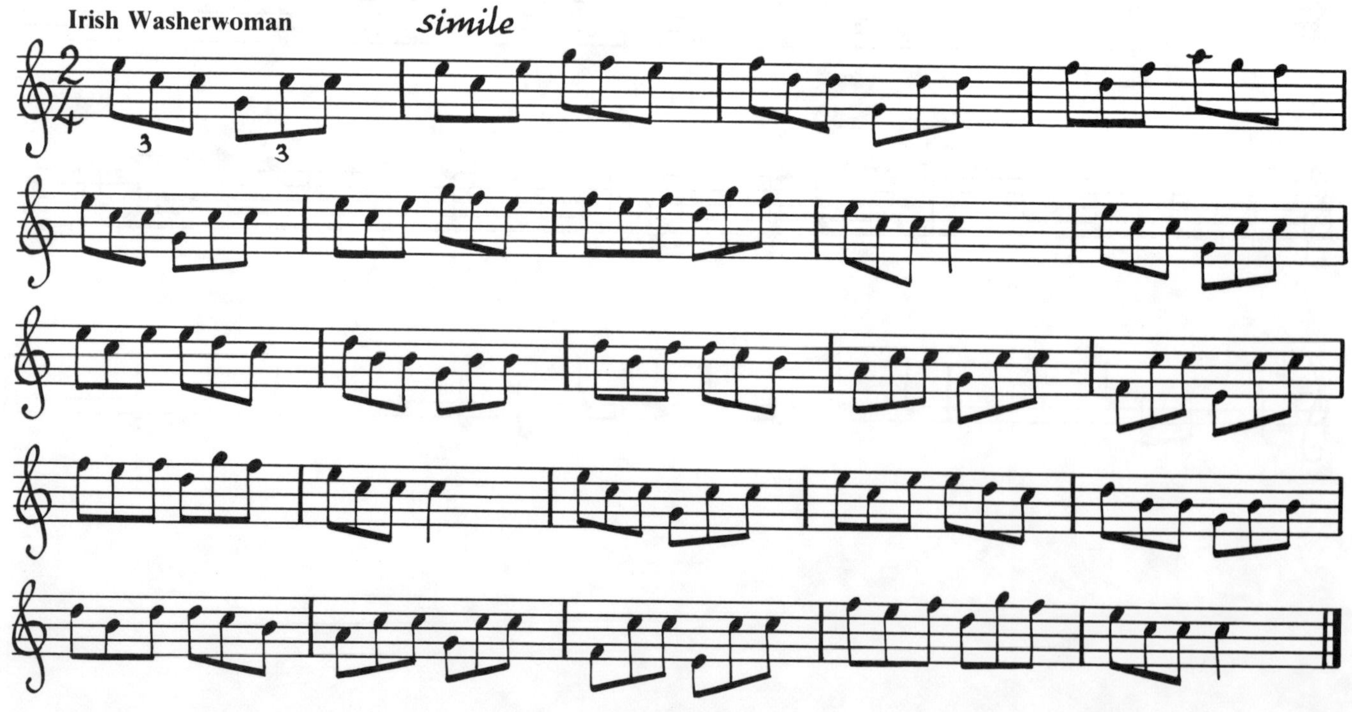

MUSIC THEORY—LESSON EIGHTEEN

THE SIXTEENTH NOTE RECEIVES ONE QUARTER BEAT

As we have learned previously, the time value of the sixteenth note is 1/4 BEAT. This means that the sixteenth note is sustained for the time required to complete the first or second half of the down beat, or the first or second half of the up beat of the foot. Four consecutive sixteenth notes comprise one beat—two notes on the down beat and two notes on the up beat.

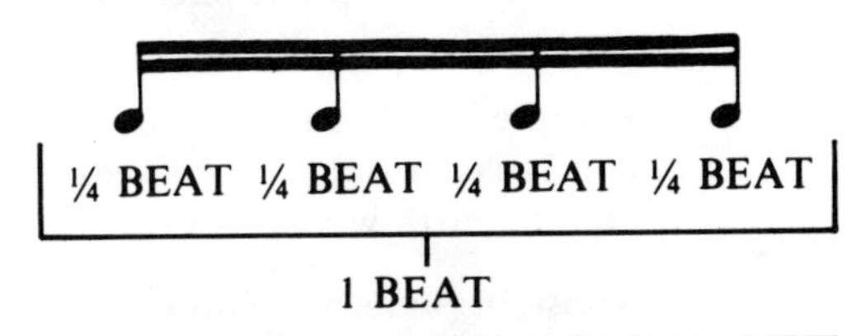

HOW TO PERFORM FOUR SIXTEENTH NOTES

To perform four sixteenth notes, one beat of the foot (down beat plus up beat) is divided into four equal parts.

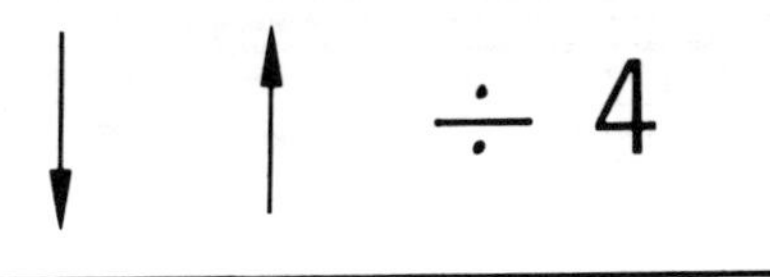

The first note is sung as the foot executes the down beat. The second note is sung while the foot remains at rest upon the floor. The third note is sung during the up beat of the foot. The fourth note is sung while the foot remains stationary at the top of its beat.

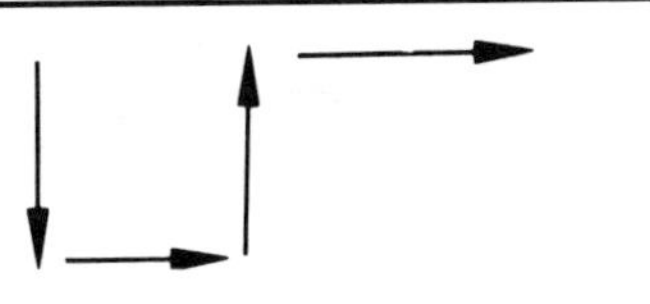

Before attempting the performance of four consecutive sixteenth notes, the student can acquire the "feel" of this new rhythm pattern by beating the foot while saying a four-syllable word such as MIS-SIS-SIP-PI. The first syllable is spoken during the down beat. The second syllable is spoken while the foot is at rest upon the floor. The third syllable is spoken during the up beat of the foot. The fourth syllable is spoken while the foot remains stationary at the top of its beat.

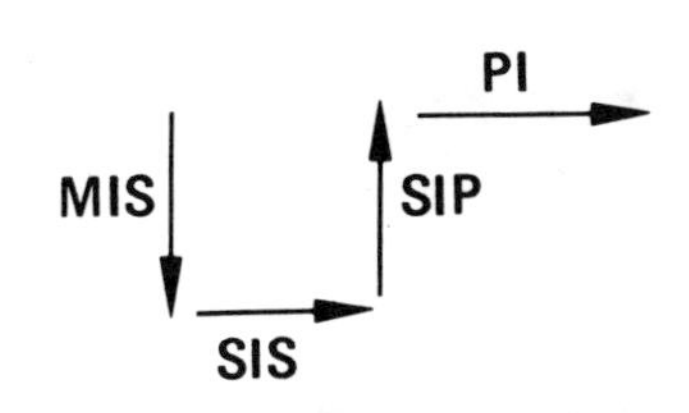

TWO SIXTEENTH NOTES FOLLOWED BY AN EIGHTH NOTE

Each sixteenth note receives 1/4 beat. The eighth note receives 1/2 beat. Together, the two sixteenth notes and the eighth note receive a total of one beat.

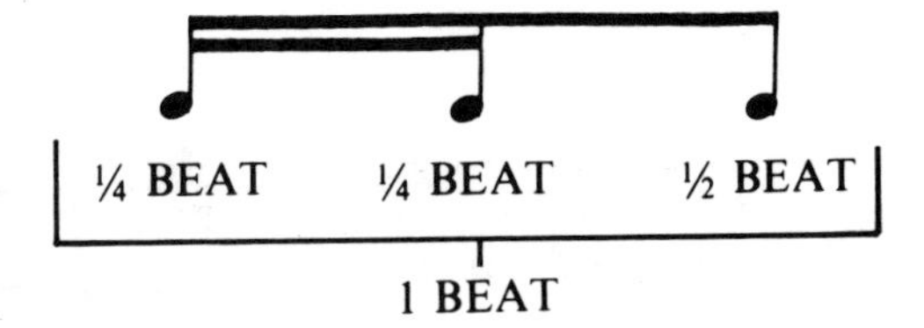

The first sixteenth note is sung during the down beat of the foot. The second sixteenth note is sung while the foot remains at rest on the floor. The eighth note is sung during the up beat of the foot plus the time the foot remains stationary at the top of its beat.

To acquire the proper rhythm for this pattern, sing the words JINGLE BELLS.

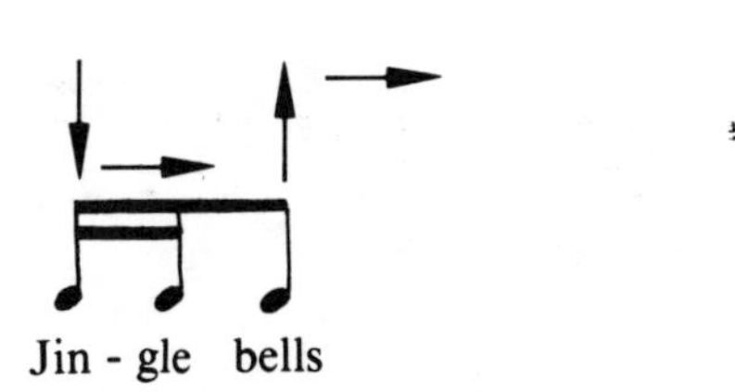

THE EIGHTH NOTE FOLLOWED BY TWO SIXTEENTH NOTES

The eighth note receives 1/2 beat. Each sixteenth note receives 1/4 beat. Together, the eighth note and two sixteenth notes receive a total of one beat.

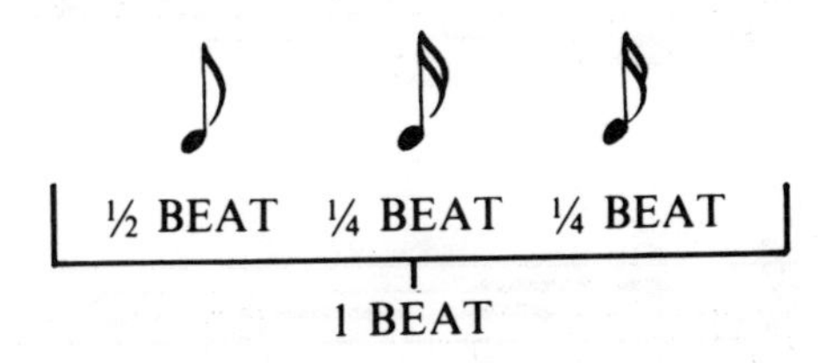

The eighth note is sung during the down beat plus the time the foot is at rest on the floor. The first sixteenth note is sung during the up beat of the foot. The second sixteenth note is sung while the foot remains stationary at the top of its beat.

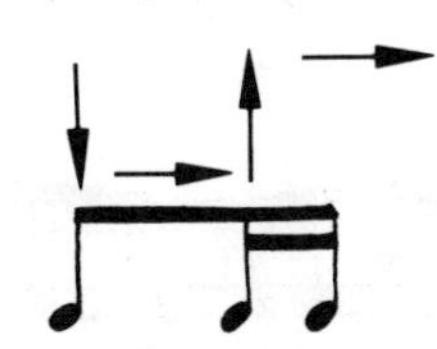

ASSIGNMENT ONE: At least two successive times each day, name each of the notes appearing in the following exercise.

ASSIGNMENT TWO: At least once each day, sing the following exercise while beating time. Sing the syllable "LA" on one pitch throughout for each of the notes. Select any pitch that feels comfortable. Sing softly and without the slightest trace of strain.

Because of the complexity of this assignment, it may be extended over a period of four weeks. Lines 1, 2 and 3 may be sung the first week; lines 4 and 5 the second week; lines 6 and 7 the third week; lines 8, 9 and 10 the fourth week.

Exercise In Sixteenth Notes

MUSIC THEORY—LESSON NINETEEN

THE "C" MAJOR SCALE

The C Major Scale consists of a series of notes beginning with the note "C," and proceeding through the musical alphabet until "C" recurs. The scale may ascend or descend.

The first note and the eighth note of the scale have the same letter name. The distance between these two notes is called an "OCTAVE."

Each note of the scale is called a "DEGREE." The degrees of the scale are numbered from one through eight.

Never in a Major Scale will two notes of the same letter occur in succession, nor will a letter of the musical alphabet be skipped in ascending or descending the scale.

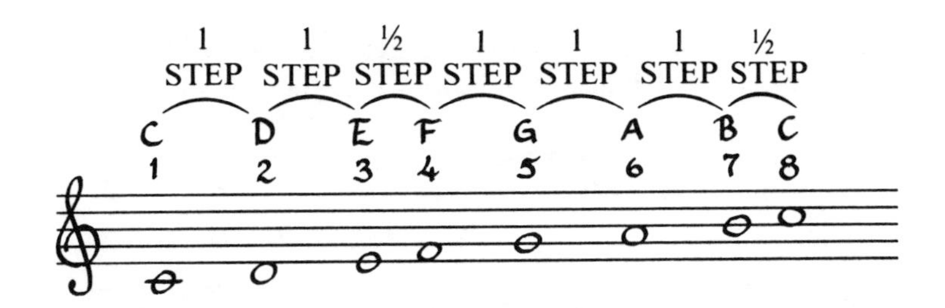

The notes "E" and "F," and "B" and "C," are one half step apart. The other adjacent notes are one step apart. As a result, the third and fourth, and the seventh and eighth, degrees of the scale are one half step apart. The other adjacent degrees are one step apart.

KEY—TONIC—KEY NOTE

In every melody there is a "home note," to which the music will resolve and come to rest (conclude). This note, toward which the melody tends to gravitate is called the "KEY NOTE" or the "TONIC."

The key note bears the same letter name as the "KEY" of the music.

For example, when the key note is "C," the selection is in the KEY OF C MAJOR and is composed of notes which occur in the C Major Scale. When the key note is "G," the selection is in the KEY OF G MAJOR, and is composed of notes which occur in the G Major Scale*. It is the scale from which the notes of the selection are derived that determines which note is the key note, thereby establishing the key of the selection.

The Major Scale may begin on any given tone, therefore any tone may be the tonic of a Major Scale.

WHY ARE KEYS NECESSARY?

If all music were in only one key, some selections would be too high or too low for the vocal range of many vocalists. By selecting the most comfortable key for each song, the singer is able to choose the key that is suited to his or her vocal range.

*Minor scales are covered in Lesson Twenty-Eight.

CONSTRUCTING MAJOR SCALES

Using the C Major Scale as a pattern, we may construct all other Major Scales.

CONSTRUCTING THE "G" MAJOR SCALE

Begin with the note "G," and proceed through the musical alphabet until "G" reoccurs.

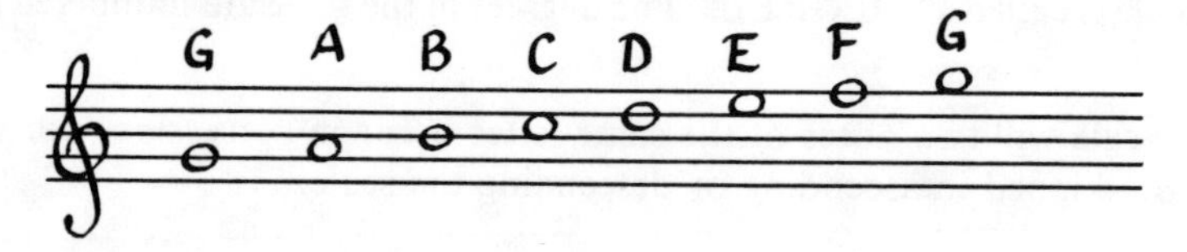

Number each degree of the scale and place horizontal brackets above the third and fourth degrees, and the seventh and eighth degrees. The brackets indicate where the half steps are to occur in the scale.

Degrees one and two are to be one step apart. "G" and "A" are one step apart.

Degrees two and three are to be one step apart. "A" and "B" are one step apart.

Degrees three and four are to be one half step apart. "B" and "C" are one half step apart.

Degrees four and five are to be one step apart. "C" and "D" are one step apart.

Degrees five and six are to be one step apart. "D" and "E" are one step apart.

Degrees six and seven are to be one step apart. "E" and "F" are one half step apart. To increase the separation between the sixth and seventh degrees so they are one step apart, while not affecting the separations between the first six degrees, the "F" note is sharped.

Degrees seven and eight are to be one half step apart. "F#" and "G" are one half step apart.

CONSTRUCTING THE "D" MAJOR SCALE

Begin with the note "D" and proceed through the musical alphabet until "D" reoccurs.

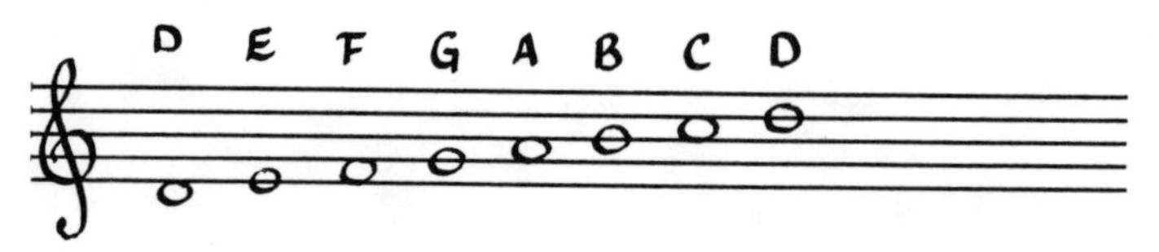

Number each degree of the scale and place horizontal brackets above the third and fourth degrees, and the seventh and eighth degrees. The brackets indicate where the half steps are to occur in the scale.

Degrees one and two are to be one step apart. "D" and "E" are one step apart.

Degrees two and three are to be one step apart. "E" and "F" are one half step apart. To increase the separation between the second and third degrees so they are one step apart, while not affecting the separation between the first two degrees, the "F" note is sharped.

Degrees three and four are to be one half step apart. "F#" and "G" are one half step apart.

Degrees four and five are to be one step apart. "G" and "A" are one step apart.

Degrees five and six are to be one step apart. "A" and "B" are one step apart.

Degrees six and seven are to be one step apart. "B" and "C" are one half step apart. To increase the separation between the sixth and seventh degrees so they are one step apart, while not affecting the separations between the first six degrees, the "C" note is sharped.

Degrees seven and eight are to be one half step apart. "C#" and "D" are one half step apart.

Because music in any given key is comprised of the notes contained in the scale of the key note, it follows that music in the Key of "G" is comprised of notes appearing in the "G" Major Scale. Music in the Key of "D" is comprised of notes appearing in the "D" Major Scale. Music in the Key of "A" is comprised of notes appearing in the "A" Major Scale, and so on.

Following are all the Major Scales.

C MAJOR C D E F G A B C

G MAJOR	G	A	B	C	D	E	F#	G
D MAJOR	D	E	F#	G	A	B	C#	D
A MAJOR	A	B	C#	D	E	F#	G#	A
E MAJOR	E	F#	G#	A	B	C#	D#	E
B MAJOR	B	C#	D#	E	F#	G#	A#	B
F# MAJOR	F#	G#	A#	B	C#	D#	E#	F#
C# MAJOR	C#	D#	E#	F#	G#	A#	B#	C#

F MAJOR	F	G	A	Bb	C	D	E	F
Bb MAJOR	Bb	C	D	Eb	F	G	A	Bb
Eb MAJOR	Eb	F	G	Ab	Bb	C	D	Eb
Ab MAJOR	Ab	Bb	C	Db	Eb	F	G	Ab
Db MAJOR	Db	Eb	F	Gb	Ab	Bb	C	Db
Gb MAJOR	Gb	Ab	Bb	Cb	Db	Eb	F	Gb
Cb MAJOR	Cb	Db	Eb	Fb	Gb	Ab	Bb	Cb

ASSIGNMENT ONE: Each day construct the fifteen scales. Compare the constructed scales with the scales above.

ASSIGNMENT TWO: Repeat the entire music theory Lesson Eighteen.

MUSIC THEORY—LESSON TWENTY

THE KEY SIGNATURE

To inform the singer and musician of the key in which a selection is to be performed, a device known as the KEY SIGNATURE is employed.

The key signature consists of sharps or flats that appear between the treble clef sign and the time signature.

The number of sharps or flats in the key signature indicates the key of the music. (See "Cycle of Fifths" below.) When neither sharps nor flats appear in the key signature, the selection is in the key of C Major.

Notes which are sharped or flatted in the key signature are to be sharped or flatted throughout the piece. For example, when the key signature contains one sharp ("F" on the fifth staff line), all "F" notes throughout the selection are to be sharped.

The key signature is usually repeated at the beginning of each line of music.

Chromatic sign(s) appearing between the treble clef sign and the time signature are called the KEY SIGNATURE.

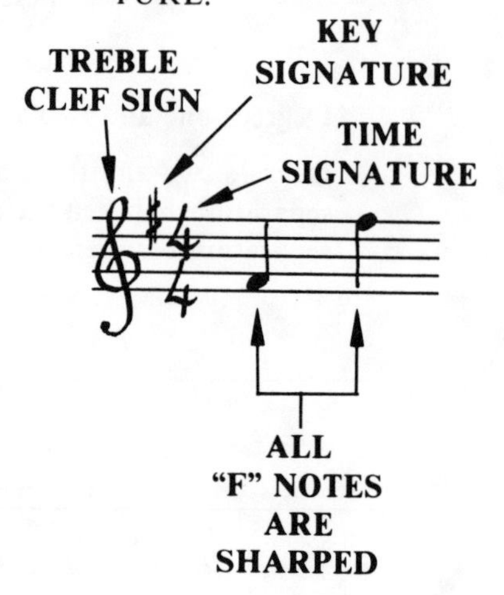

ACCIDENTALS

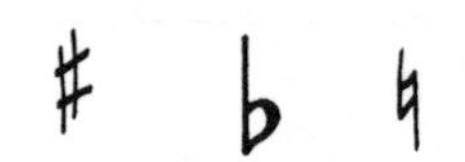

An ACCIDENTAL is a chromatic sign (sharp, flat, natural) not appearing in the key signature, which occurs before a note in a composition. While a sharp or flat in the key signature is applied throughout the piece, an accidental affects only those notes *within its measure* which follow on the same line or space of the staff.

THE CYCLE OF FIFTHS—ALSO CALLED THE CIRCLE OF FIFTHS

Following are the Major scales, beginning with C Major and progressing in order of the ascending number of sharps occurring in each scale.

C	G	D	A	E	B	F#	C#
0#	1#	2#	3#	4#	5#	6#	7#

By counting to the fifth note of any Major scale, the next scale in the progression can be determined. For example, the fifth note of the C Major scale is G. The fifth note of the G Major scale is D. The fifth note of the D Major scale is A, etc.

The scale of C# Major (the scale of 7 sharps) contains the maximum number of sharps that occur in a Major scale. However, it is theoretically possible to advance the progression of Major scales further by counting to the fifth note of the C# Major scale, and then to the fifth note of each succeeding scale, until arriving at the scale of B# Major.

C	G	D	A	E	B	F#	C#	G#	D#	A#	E#	B#
0#	1#	2#	3#	4#	5#	6#	7#	8#	9#	10#	11#	12#

Since the (theoretical) scale of B# Major is the same as the scale of C Major, because B# is the same as C, it can be observed that the progression of Major scales advances by fifths until arriving at the point from which it began.

Because the family of notes that comprises each Major scale is the same for the key of the same letter name, it follows that a knowledge of the number of sharps occurring in each scale enables the performer to determine a selection's key by observing the number of sharps that appears in the key signature.

ASSIGNMENT ONE: Memorize the order of the scales up to the scale of seven sharps, and be familiar with the number of sharps that are found in each scale.

ASSIGNMENT TWO: Answer the following questions.

QUESTIONS IN MUSIC THEORY

1. In the Key of G Major, how many sharps occur? ____
2. In the Key of C# Major, how many sharps occur? ____
3. In the Key of D Major, how many sharps occur? ____
4. In the Key of F# Major, how many sharps occur? ____
5. In the Key of A Major, how many sharps occur? ____
6. In the Key of B Major, how many sharps occur? ____
7. In the Key of E Major, how many sharps occur? ____
8. In the Key of C Major, how many sharps occur? ____

MUSIC THEORY—LESSON TWENTY-ONE

We have learned that in the Key of C Major, no sharps occur. In the Key of G Major, one sharp occurs. The Key of D Major contains two sharps. The Key of A Major contains three sharps. The Key of E Major contains four sharps. The Key of B Major contains five sharps. The Key of F# Major contains six sharps. The Key of C# Major contains seven sharps.

In this lesson the student is to become familiar with the notes that are sharped in each key.

The order of sharped notes as they occur in the Major scales (keys) is:

F# C# G# D# A# E# B#

By memorizing the order of sharps, the student will know the following.

The Key of G Major contains 1 sharp . . . F#
The Key of D Major contains 2 sharps . . F# C#
The Key of A Major contains 3 sharps . . F# C# G#
The Key of E Major contains 4 sharps . . F# C# G# D#
The Key of B Major contains 5 sharps . . F# C# G# D# A#
The Key of F# Major contains 6 sharps . F# C# G# D# A# E#
The Key of C# Major contains 7 sharps . F# C# G# D# A# E# B#

ASSIGNMENT ONE: Memorize the seven sharps in the order in which they appear in the Major scales.

ASSIGNMENT TWO: Answer the following questions.

1. In the Key of E Major, how many sharps occur?_____ Which are they? __________
2. In the Key of B Major, how many sharps occur?_____ Which are they? __________
3. In the Key of A Major, how many sharps occur?_____ Which are they? __________
4. In the Key of F# Major, how many sharps occur?_____ Which are they? __________
5. In the Key of D Major, how many sharps occur?_____ Which are they? __________
6. In the Key of C# Major, how many sharps occur?_____ Which are they? __________
7. In the Key of G Major, how many sharps occur?_____ Which are they? __________
8. In the Key of C Major, how many sharps occur?_____ Which are they? __________

MUSIC THEORY—LESSON TWENTY-TWO

Below are the Major scales progressing through the cycle of fifths.

C	G	D	A	E	B	F#	C#	G#	D#	A#	E#	B#
0#	1#	2#	3#	4#	5#	6#	7#					

By using the enharmonic names for the scales of E#, A#, D#, G#, C#, F#, and B, the number of usable scales can be extended to include seven more scales (keys), each one containing one or more flats. The names of these seven scales (keys) are F, Bb, Eb, Ab, Db, Gb, and Cb.

					7b	6b	5b	4b	3b	2b	1b	0b
					Cb	Gb	Db	Ab	Eb	Bb	F	C
C	G	D	A	E	B	F#	C#	G#	D#	A#	E#	B#
0#	1#	2#	3#	4#	5#	6#	7#					

Following are the flat scales, beginning with F Major and progressing in order of the ascending number of flats occurring in each scale.

F	Bb	Eb	Ab	Db	Gb	Cb
1b	2b	3b	4b	5b	6b	7b

ASSIGNMENT ONE: Memorize the order of the flat scales, and be familiar with the number of flats that are found in each scale.

ASSIGNMENT TWO: Answer the following questions.

QUESTIONS IN MUSIC THEORY

1. In the key of F Major, how many flats occur? _____
2. In the key of Cb Major, how many flats occur?_____
3. In the key of Bb Major, how many flats occur?_____
4. In the key of Gb Major, how many flats occur?_____
5. In the key of Eb Major, how many flats occur?_____
6. In the key of Db Major, how many flats occur?_____
7. In the key of Ab Major, how many flats occur?_____
8. In the key of C Major, how many flats occur? _____

MUSIC THEORY—LESSON TWENTY-THREE

For this lesson the student will become familiar with the notes that are flatted in each key. The order of flatted notes as they occur in the Major scales (keys) is:

Bb Eb Ab Db Gb Cb Fb

Notice that the order of flats is the reverse of the order of sharps—F# C# G# D# A# E# B#.

By memorizing the order of flats, the student will know the following.

The Key of F Major contains 1 flat . . . Bb
The Key of Bb Major contains 2 flats . Bb Eb
The Key of Eb Major contains 3 flats . Bb Eb Ab
The Key of Ab Major contains 4 flats . Bb Eb Ab Db
The Key of Db Major contains 5 flats. Bb Eb Ab Db Gb
The Key of Gb Major contains 6 flats . Bb Eb Ab Db Gb Cb
The Key of Cb Major contains 7 flats . Bb Eb Ab Db Gb Cb Fb

ASSIGNMENT ONE: Memorize the seven flats in the order in which they appear in the Major scales.

ASSIGNMENT TWO: Answer the following questions.

1. In the Key of Ab Major, how many flats occur? ____ Which are they?________________
2. In the Key of Db Major, how many flats occur? ____ Which are they?________________
3. In the Key of Eb Major, how many flats occur? ____ Which are they?________________
4. In the Key of Gb Major, how many flats occur? ____ Which are they?________________
5. In the Key of Bb Major, how many flats occur? ____ Which are they?________________
6. In the Key of Cb Major, how many flats occur? ____ Which are they?________________
7. In the Key of F Major, how many flats occur?____ Which are they?________________
8. In the Key of C Major, how many flats occur? ____ Which are they?________________

MUSIC THEORY—LESSON TWENTY-FOUR

The C Major Scale contains no Sharps and no Flats.

The G Major Scale contains 1 Sharp . . . F#
The D Major Scale contains 2 Sharps . . F# C#
The A Major Scale contains 3 Sharps . . F# C# G#
The E Major Scale contains 4 Sharps . . F# C# G# D#
The B Major Scale contains 5 Sharps . . F# C# G# D# A#
The F# Major Scale contains 6 Sharps . F# C# G# D# A# E#
The C# Major Scale contains 7 Sharps . F# C# G# D# A# E# B#

The F Major Scale contains 1 Flat . . . . Bb
The Bb Major Scale contains 2 Flats . . . Bb Eb
The Eb Major Scale contains 3 Flats . . . Bb Eb Ab
The Ab Major Scale contains 4 Flats . . Bb Eb Ab Db
The Db Major Scale contains 5 Flats . . Bb Eb Ab Db Gb
The Gb Major Scale contains 6 Flats . . Bb Eb Ab Db Gb Cb
The Cb Major Scale contains 7 Flats . . Bb Eb Ab Db Gb Cb Fb

In printed music, the fifteen key signatures appear as shown below.

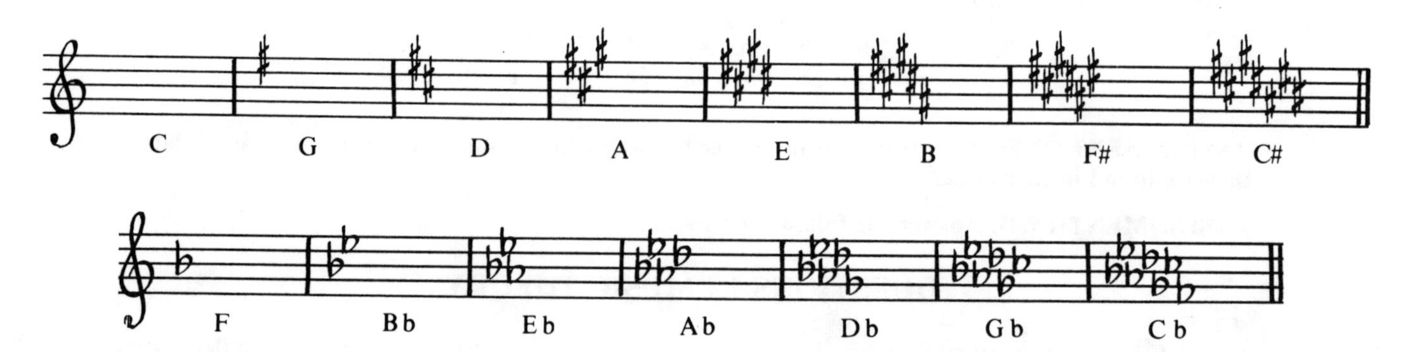

ASSIGNMENT ONE: Memorize all the information on the preceding page and answer the following questions. The answers are to be written on a separate sheet of paper, once each day.

ASSIGNMENT TWO: Begin a thorough review of all Music Theory covered up to this point.

QUESTIONS IN MUSIC THEORY

1. In the Key of G, how many sharps occur? ________ Which are they?________________
2. In the Key of F, how many flats occur? ________ Which are they?________________
3. In the Key of Db, how many flats occur? ________ Which are they?________________
4. In the Key of Gb, how many flats occur? ________ Which are they?________________
5. In the Key of F#, how many sharps occur? ________ Which are they?________________
6. In the Key of Ab, how many flats occur? ________ Which are they?________________
7. In the Key of C#, how many sharps occur? ________ Which are they?________________
8. In the Key of B, how many sharps occur? ________ Which are they?________________
9. In the Key of A, how many sharps occur? ________ Which are they?________________
10. In the Key of Bb, how many flats occur? ________ Which are they?________________
11. In the Key of E, how many sharps occur? ________ Which are they?________________
12. In the Key of D, how many sharps occur? ________ Which are they?________________
13. In the Key of Eb, how many flats occur? ________ Which are they?________________
14. In the Key of Cb, how many flats occur? ________ Which are they?________________
15. In the Key of 1 flat, which note is flatted?________________________________
16. In the Key of 1 sharp, which note is sharped? ________________________________
17. In the Key of 2 flats, which notes are flatted?________________________________
18. In the Key of 2 sharps, which notes are sharped? ________________________________
19. In the Key of 3 flats, which notes are flatted?________________________________
20. In the Key of 3 sharps, which notes are sharped?________________________________
21. In the Key of 4 flats, which notes are flatted?________________________________
22. In the Key of 4 sharps, which notes are sharped?________________________________
23. In the Key of 5 flats, which notes are flatted?________________________________
24. In the Key of 5 sharps, which notes are sharped?________________________________
25. In the Key of 6 flats, which notes are flatted?________________________________
26. In the Key of 6 sharps, which notes are sharped?________________________________
27. In the Key of 7 flats, which notes are flatted?________________________________
28. In the Key of 7 sharps, which notes are sharped?________________________________

MUSIC THEORY—LESSON TWENTY-FIVE

CHORDS

When three or more different notes are produced at the same time, the resultant sound is called a CHORD.

Every chord is given a name, such as G Major, C Major, D Dominant Seventh, G Dominant Seventh, A minor, D minor.

The chord name is referred to as a CHORD SYMBOL.

In printed music, all Major chords are indicated by their letter name only. Therefore, G Major is called "G," C Major is called "C," etc.

Dominant Seventh chords appear as their letter name followed by the number "7," such as D7, G7, etc.

Minor chords are shown by their letter name, followed by the small letter "m," such as Am, Dm, etc.

Each chord is derived from a Major scale that bears the same letter name as the chord. Chords such as D Major, D minor, D augmented, D diminished, D Seventh, etc., are all derived from the D Major scale. Chords such as C Major, C minor, C augmented, C diminished, C Seventh, etc., are all derived from the C Major scale, etc.

The most basic chord type is called a TRIAD *(TRY-add)*. The triad contains three different notes. There are four kinds of triads. They are the MAJOR TRIAD, MINOR TRIAD, AUGMENTED TRIAD, DIMINISHED TRIAD. In current usage, the four triads are called the MAJOR CHORD, MINOR CHORD, AUGMENTED CHORD, DIMINISHED CHORD.

The Major chord is derived from the 1st, 3rd, and 5th notes of the Major Scale.

The Minor chord is derived from the 1st, flatted 3rd, and 5th notes of the Major Scale.

The Augmented chord is derived from the 1st, 3rd, and sharped 5th notes of the Major Scale.

The Diminished chord is derived from the 1st, flatted 3rd, and flatted 5th notes of the Major Scale.

The letter name of a chord is the same as the first note of the scale from which the chord is derived. The letter name of a chord is called the ROOT.

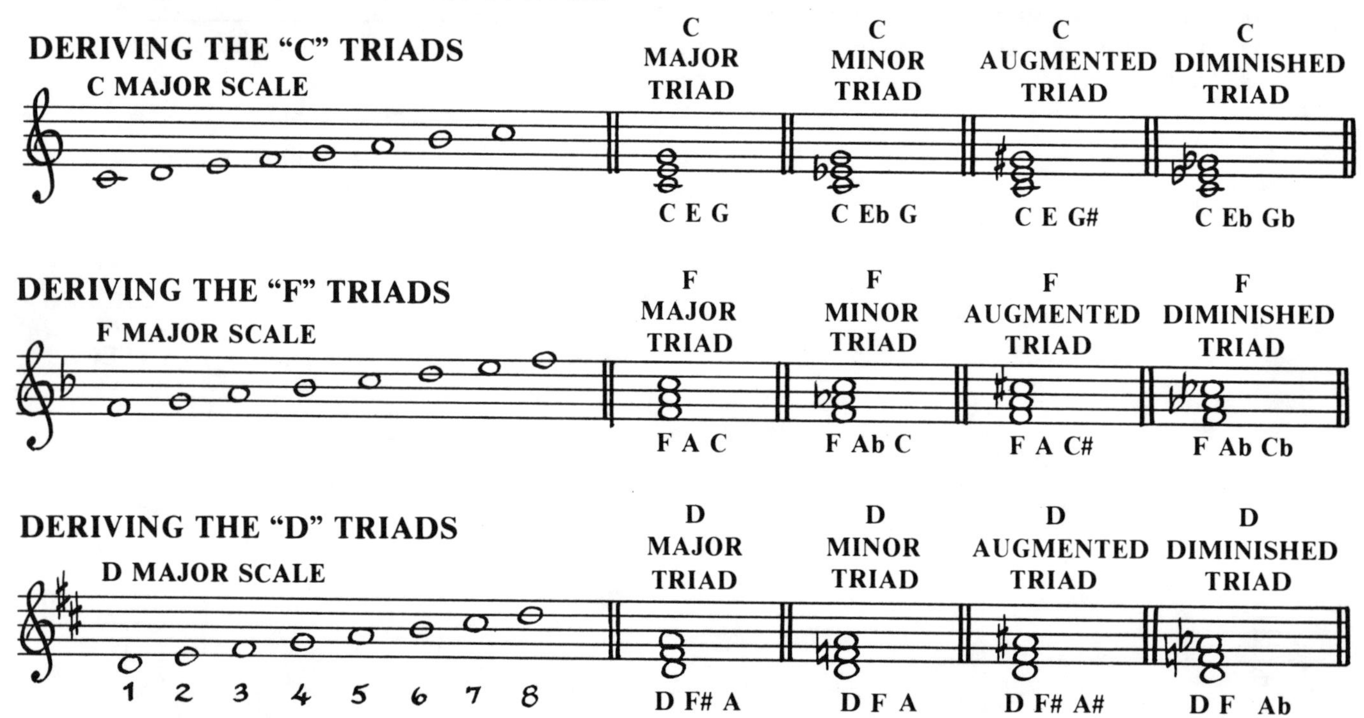

ASSIGNMENT ONE: Construct the fifteen Major Scales.

C Major	A Major	F# Major	Bb Major	Db Major
G Major	E Major	C# Major	Eb Major	Gb Major
D Major	B Major	F Major	Ab Major	Cb Major

Next, derive the four triads from each Major Scale. This is to be done once each day.

ASSIGNMENT TWO: Memorize the following chord derivation formulas.

Major	1	3	5	
Minor	1	b3	5	
Augmented	1	3	#5	
Diminished	1	b3	b5	
Major Sixth	1	3	5	6
Minor Sixth	1	b3	5	6

Major Seventh	1	3	5	7	
Dominant Seventh	1	3	5	b7	
Minor Seventh	1	b3	5	b7	
Diminished Seventh	1	b3	b5	bb7	
Augmented Seventh	1	3	#5	b7	
Dominant Ninth	1	3	5	b7	9

MUSIC THEORY—LESSON TWENTY-SIX

INTERVALS

An INTERVAL is the distance in pitch between any two tones. If the two tones are sounded simultaneously, the interval is called a HARMONIC INTERVAL. If the two tones are sounded in succession, the interval is called a MELODIC INTERVAL.

HARMONIC INTERVAL MELODIC INTERVAL

When two voices or instruments sound the same tone, it is referred to as a "UNISON" or a "PERFECT PRIME."

To determine intervals, the Major Scale is employed as a measuring stick.

The distance from the Tonic to the Second Degree of the Major scale is called an interval of a second. The Tonic to the Third Degree is called an interval of a third. The Tonic to the Fourth Degree is called an interval of a fourth, etc.

PERFECT INTERVALS AND MAJOR INTERVALS

The intervals from the Tonic to the Fourth Degree, Tonic to the Fifth Degree, Tonic to the Octave of all Major Scales are called "PERFECT INTERVALS." Memorize the perfect intervals as intervals of 4, 5 and 8.

The remaining intervals—that is, from the Tonic to the Second Degree, Tonic to the Third Degree, Tonic to the Sixth Degree, Tonic to the Seventh Degree—of all Major Scales are called "MAJOR INTERVALS." Memorize the major intervals as intervals of 2, 3, 6, 7.

AUGMENTED INTERVALS

When a Major Interval or a Perfect Interval is chromatically increased a half step, it becomes an "AUGMENTED INTERVAL."

THE MINOR INTERVAL

When a Major Interval is chromatically decreased a half step, it becomes a "MINOR INTERVAL."

ASSIGNMENT ONE: Carefully study the information appearing in this lesson.

ASSIGNMENT TWO: Answer the questions appearing below.

QUESTIONS IN MUSIC THEORY

Which note is a minor second higher than C? ____________
Which note is a major second higher than D? ____________
Which note is a minor third higher than F? ____________
Which note is a major third higher than F? ____________
Which note is a perfect fourth higher than G? ____________
Which note is an augmented fourth higher than G? ____________
Which note is a perfect fifth higher than A? ____________
Which note is an augmented fifth higher than A? ____________
Which note is a major sixth higher than G? ____________
Which note is a minor sixth higher than G? ____________
Which note is a minor seventh higher than D? ____________
Which note is a major seventh higher than D? ____________
Which note is an octave higher than E? ____________
Which note is a major second higher than A? ____________
Which note is a major second higher than D? ____________
Which note is a minor second higher than D? ____________
Which note is a major second higher than E? ____________
Which note is a minor second higher than E? ____________
Which note is a major second higher than B? ____________
Which note is a minor second higher than B? ____________
Which note is a major third higher than C? ____________
Which note is a minor third higher than C? ____________
Which note is a major third higher than A? ____________
Which note is a minor third higher than A? ____________
Which note is a major third higher than E? ____________
Which note is a minor third higher than E? ____________
Which note is a perfect fourth higher than F? ____________
Which note is a perfect fourth higher than Bb? ____________
Which note is a perfect fourth higher than G? ____________
Which note is a perfect fifth higher than Eb? ____________
Which note is a perfect fifth higher than Ab? ____________
Which note is a perfect fifth higher than B? ____________
Which note is a major sixth higher than D? ____________
Which note is an augmented sixth higher than C? ____________
Which note is an augmented second higher than G? ____________

MUSIC THEORY—LESSON TWENTY-SEVEN

THE DIMINISHED INTERVAL

When a Minor Interval or a Perfect Interval is chromatically decreased a half step, it becomes a "DIMINISHED INTERVAL."

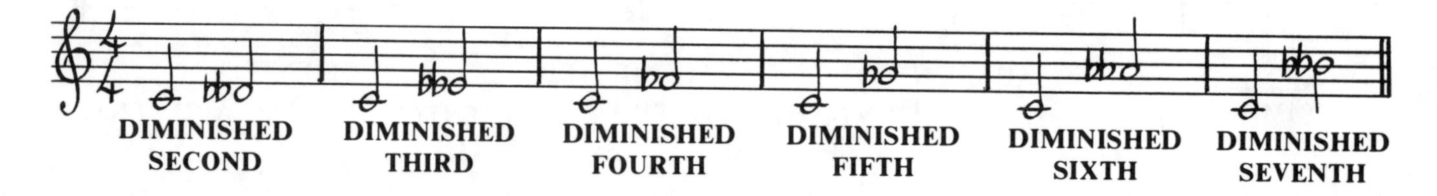

This covers in full the five interval types—Major, Minor, Perfect, Augmented, Diminished. Some intervals are purely theoretical and never referred to in ordinary use; for example, the diminished second and the augmented third.

Following is a listing of all the intervals derived from the C Major Scale. The purely theoretical intervals have been excluded. Included are intervals greater than an octave. Intervals of a Ninth are treated as Seconds, Tenths as Thirds, Elevenths as Fourths, Twelfths as Fifths, Thirteenths as Sixths.

TABLE OF INTERVALS

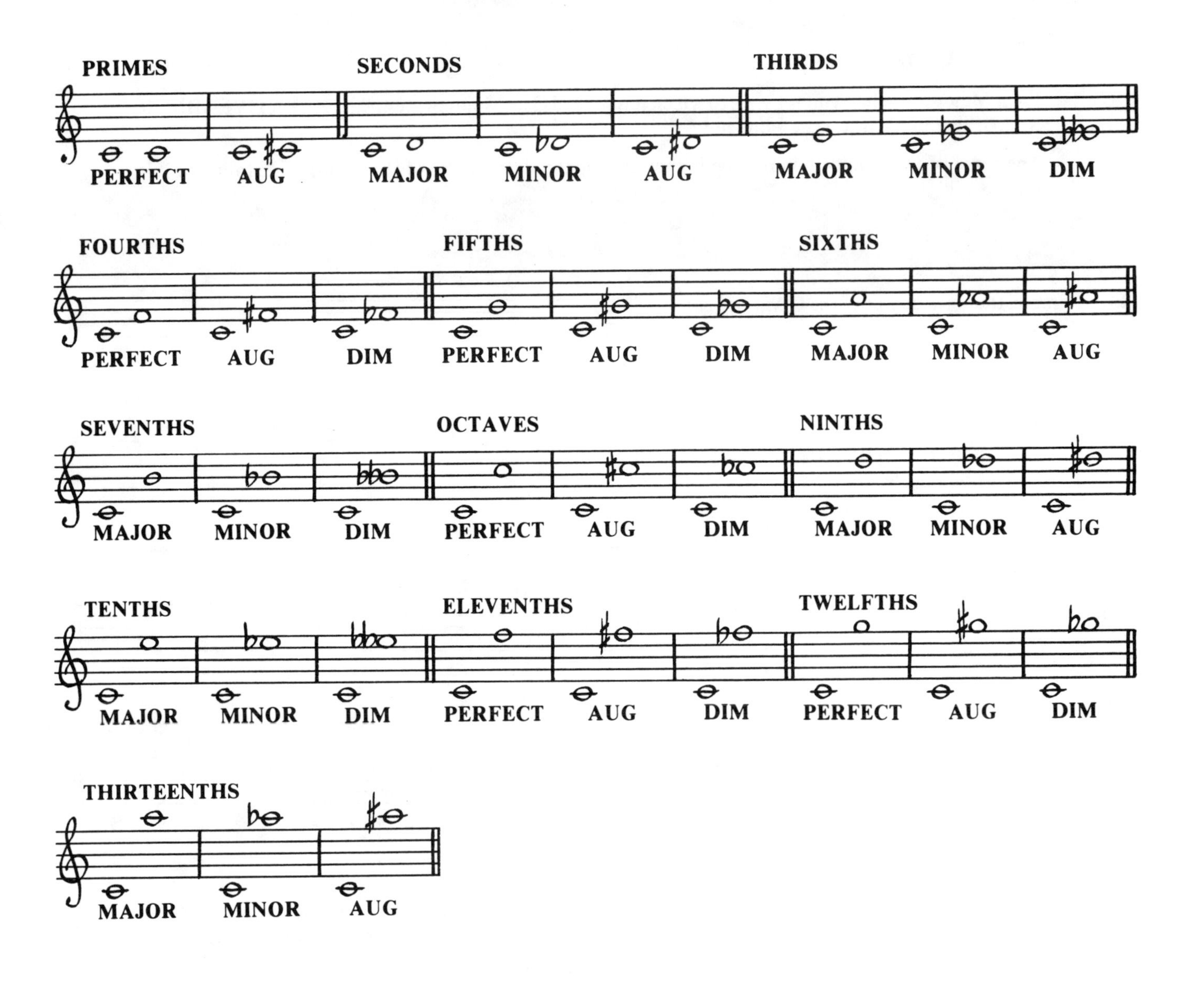

ASSIGNMENT ONE: Carefully study the information appearing in this lesson.

ASSIGNMENT TWO: Write the type name and the number name for each of the intervals appearing in the Interval Drill. This is to be written on a separate sheet of paper, once each day.

INTERVAL DRILL

MUSIC THEORY—LESSON TWENTY-EIGHT

THE MINOR SCALE

Each Major Scale has a minor scale to which it is related. The Major Scale and its RELATIVE MINOR SCALE contain exactly the same notes.

The tonic of the relative minor scale is the same as the sixth degree of the Major scale to which it is related.

For example, the sixth degree of the C Major Scale is "A."

From the "A" note the Relative Minor Scale is built (the "A" Minor Scale).

The sixth degree of the G Major Scale is "E."

From the "E" note the Relative Minor Scale is built (the "E" Minor Scale).

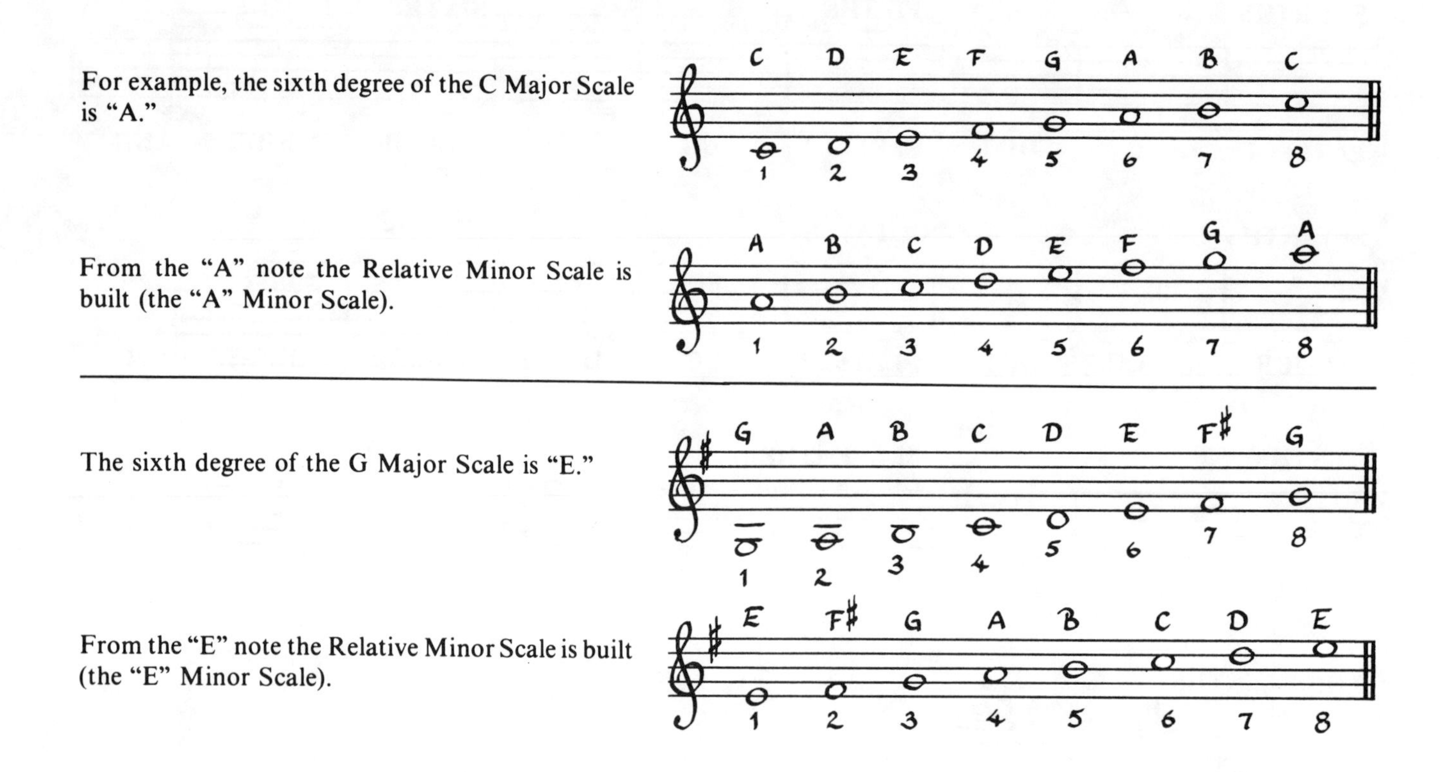

The key signature of the Major scale and its Relative Minor scale are the same. However, in the Major scale the half steps occur between 3 and 4, and 7 and 8. In the Relative Minor scale, the half steps occur between 2 and 3, and 5 and 6.

The Minor scales constructed above are called NATURAL MINOR SCALES.

THE HARMONIC MINOR SCALE

If the seventh degree of the Natural Minor Scale is raised a half step, it then becomes a HARMONIC MINOR SCALE.

THE "A" HARMONIC MINOR SCALE

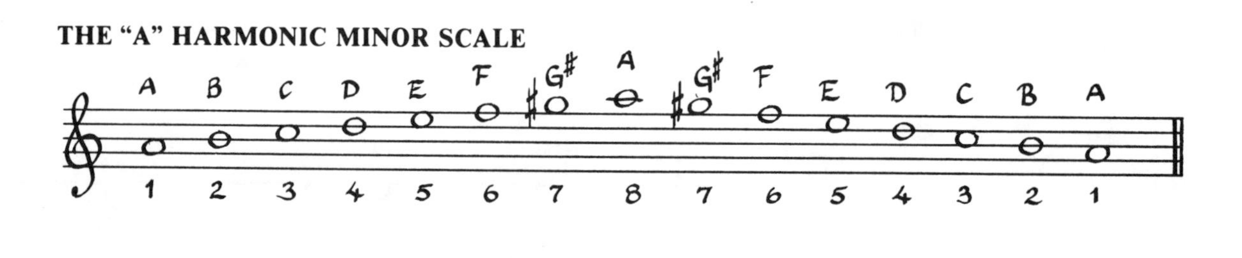

THE "E" HARMONIC MINOR SCALE

THE MELODIC MINOR SCALE

If the Sixth and Seventh degrees of the natural Minor Scale are raised one half step when ascending and then lowered to their normal Natural Minor position when descending, the newly created scale is called the MELODIC MINOR SCALE.

THE "A" MELODIC MINOR SCALE

THE "E" MELODIC MINOR SCALE

It is not unusual for all three forms of the minor scale (Natural, Harmonic, Melodic) to be utilized in the melody or harmony of a selection.

Since each key signature represents both the Major Key and its Relative Minor Key—all three minor key forms share the same key signature—other indicators must be sought to determine the specific key. A quick and easy way to verify the key is to glance at the last note of the selection. Since the last note is usually the key note, this is an excellent means to establish the key of a selection. For example, if the key signature contains one flat ("B" flat), the key is either F Major or D Minor. If the key note is "D," it is safe to assume that the music is written in the Key of D Minor.

CHANGING MUSIC FROM A MAJOR KEY TO A MINOR KEY

Each Major Scale can be made into a Harmonic Minor Scale of the same Tonic name by lowering the third and sixth degrees of the Major Scale, one half step.

If a selection is written in a Major Key and it is desired to change the melody to minor, this is accomplished by lowering each third degree note and each sixth degree note, one half step.

Major Scales and Minor Scales with the same Tonic are called "PARALLEL" Major and Minor scales.

Below are the Key Signatures for the Major Keys and their Relative Minor Keys.

ASSIGNMENT: Using music manuscript paper, write each Major Scale and its Key Signature. Below each Major Scale, write its Relative Natural Minor Scale, ascending and descending. Below this, write the Relative Harmonic Minor Scale, ascending and descending. Below this, write the Relative Melodic Minor Scale, ascending and descending.

The Major scales are C Major, G Major, D Major, A Major, E Major, B Major, F# Major, C# Major, F Major, Bb Major, Eb Major, Ab Major, Db Major, Gb Major, Cb Major.

When writing the Melodic Minor Scales, employ sharps, flats and naturals as necessary to indicate the unaltered sixth and seventh degrees of the descending scale.

This assignment is to be performed once each day. An example appears below.

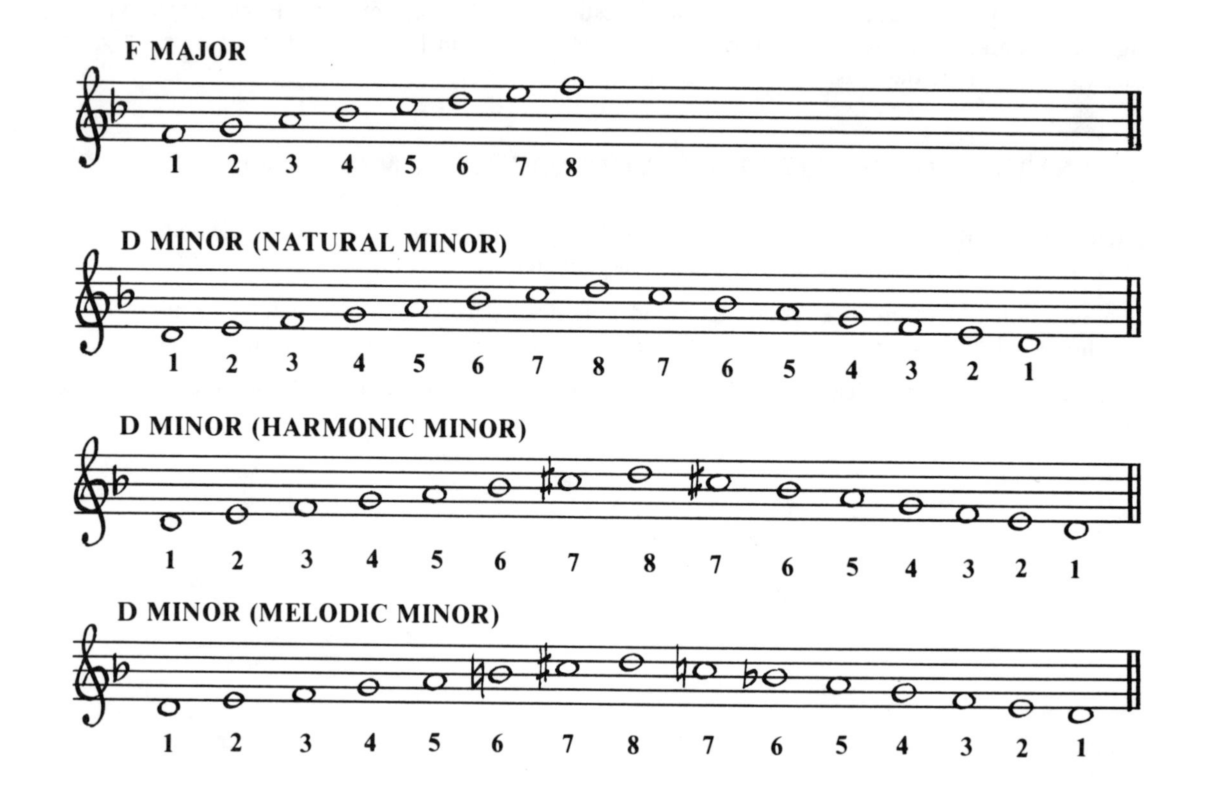

MUSIC THEORY—LESSON TWENTY-NINE

INVERSION OF INTERVALS

The INVERSION of an interval is the reversing of the two notes forming the interval, so that the lower note becomes the higher and the higher note the lower. This is accomplished by raising the lower note an octave, or else lowering the upper note an octave.

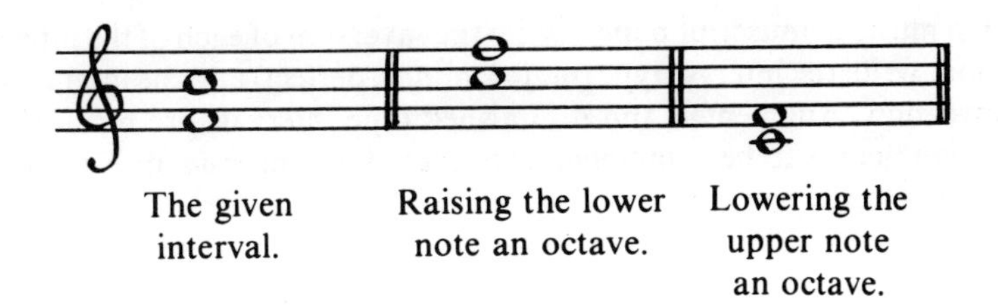

The given interval. | Raising the lower note an octave. | Lowering the upper note an octave.

A Perfect Fourth, when inverted, becomes a Perfect Fifth. A Perfect Fifth, when inverted, becomes a Perfect Fourth. The total is always nine.

When a Perfect Interval is inverted, it remains Perfect. For example, "C" to "F" is a Perfect Fourth, and "F" to "C" is a Perfect Fifth. Notice that the given interval and its inversion total "nine."

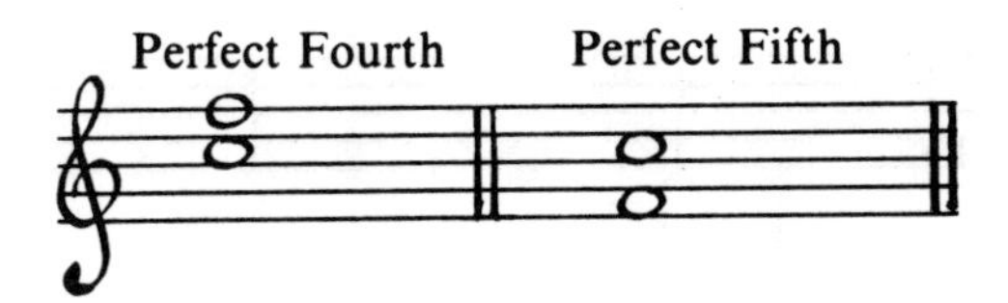

A Major Interval, when inverted, becomes a Minor Interval. A Minor Interval, when inverted, becomes a Major Interval. The total is always nine.

When a Major Interval is inverted, it becomes Minor. For example, "C" to "E" is a Major Third, and "E" to "C" is a Minor Sixth. Notice that the given interval and its inversion total "nine."

When a Minor Interval is inverted, it becomes Major. For example, "D" to "C" is a Minor Seventh, and "C" to "D" is a Major Second. Notice that the given interval and its inversion total "nine."

An Augmented Interval, when inverted, becomes a Diminished Interval. A Diminished Interval, when inverted, becomes an Augmented Interval. The total is always nine.

When an Augmented Interval is inverted, it becomes Diminished. For example, "C" to "F#" is an Augmented Fourth, and "F#" to "C" is a Diminished Fifth. Notice that the given interval and its inversion total "nine."

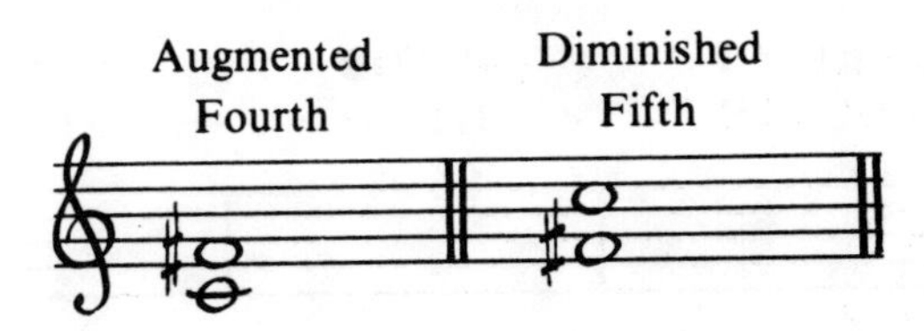

When a Diminished Interval is inverted, it becomes Augmented. For example, "D" to "Gb" is a Diminished Fourth, and "Gb" to "D" is an Augmented Fifth. Notice that the given interval and its inversion total "nine."

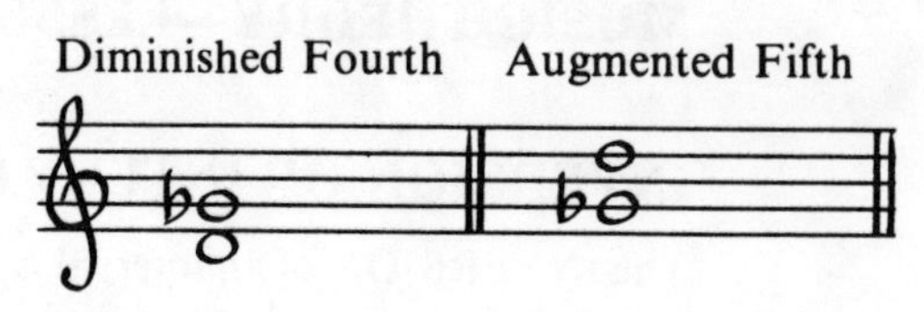

ASSIGNMENT: On music manuscript paper, write the inversion of each of the intervals shown below. Above each inversion, write the interval type (major, minor, perfect) and the interval number (2nd, 3rd, 4th, etc.) of the inversion. Augmented and diminished type intervals are not included in the lesson assignment. The assignment is to be completed once each day. The student is to compare his answers with those appearing below.

INTERVAL STUDY

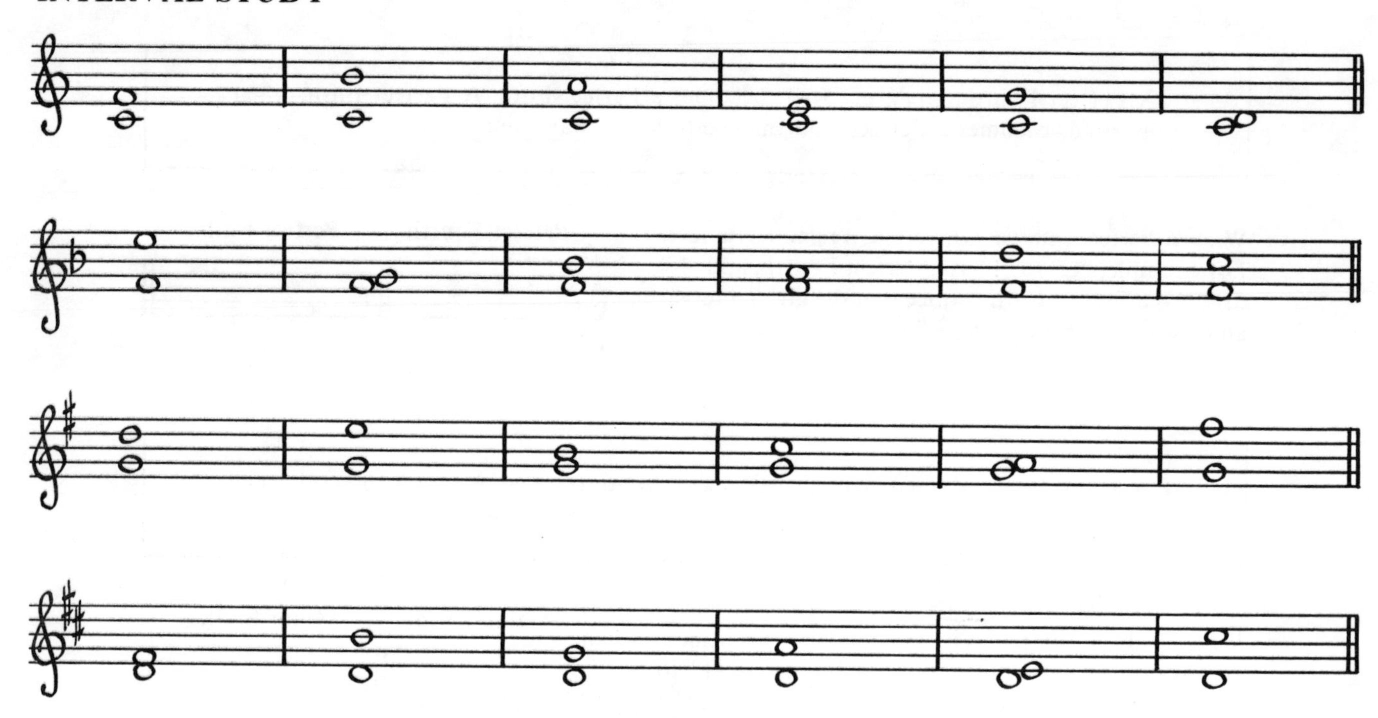

ANSWERS

MUSIC THEORY—LESSON THIRTY

TESSITURA *(tess-see-TOO-rah)*

TESSITURA refers to the general range of a vocal part, excluding a few isolated high or low notes. This term is used with regard to how a vocal part "feels" to the singer.

TRANSPOSITION

For a song to be comfortably within the range of the voice it may be necessary to change its key to another that is more suitable. TRANSPOSITION means to change the key of a selection.

There are several ways to transpose music. Perhaps the easiest for the singer is a system using SOLMIZATION. The subject of solmization is covered in considerable detail in SECTION THREE—SIGHT SINGING.

TRANSPOSING BY NUMBER

Write the Major Scales of the present key and the key to which you would like to transpose. If, for example, the music is in the Key of F Major, and you would like to transpose to the Key of G Major, write the F Major Scale and the G Major Scale.

Next, number the degrees of both scales.

Now, on the sheet of music that is to be transposed *(Merrily We Roll Along,* below), number each of the notes so they correspond with the numbers of the degrees of the F Major Scale. Finally, to complete the transposition, rewrite the selection by referring to the numbers of the G Major Scale. Make adjustments for notes having accidentals.

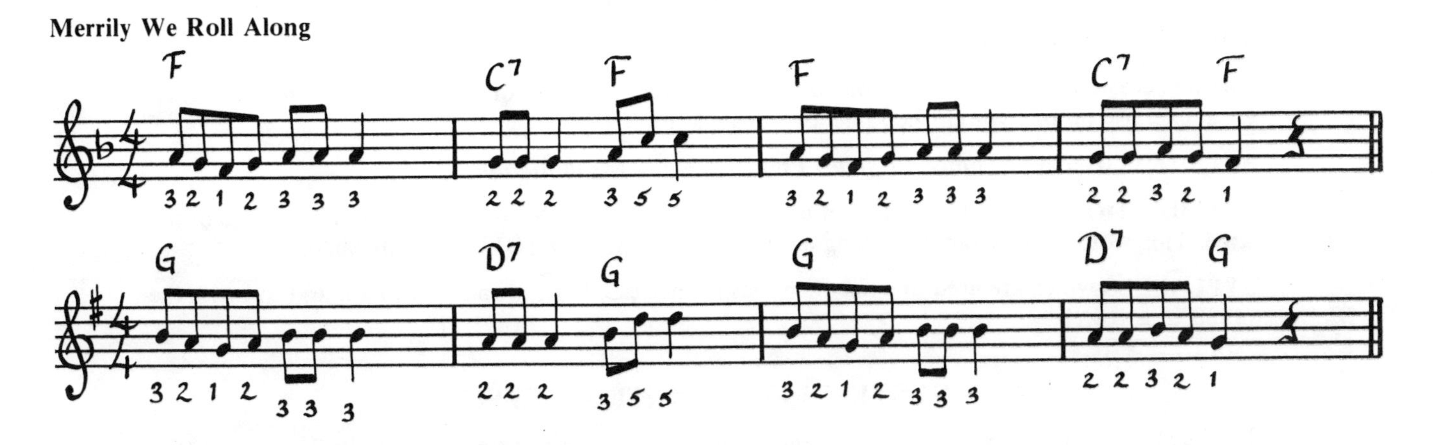

TRANSPOSING BY INTERVALS

Determine the interval from the present key to the key to which you would like to transpose. In the example above, the distance from the Key of F Major to the Key of G Major is an interval of a Major Second. Therefore, to transpose from the Key of F Major to the Key of G Major, each note is to be raised an interval of a Major Second.

When transposing by intervals, it is frequently more difficult transposing down than transposing up. To simplify a downward transposition, it may be helpful to use inversions. Rather than transpose down a Minor Third, transpose up a Major Sixth. Rather than transpose down a Perfect Fifth, transpose up a Perfect Fourth. Rather than transpose down a Diminished Fourth, transpose up an Augmented Fifth. When using inversions to transpose, the transposed notes are to be lowered one octave.

ASSIGNMENT ONE: Experiment with transposition.

ASSIGNMENT TWO: Review all lessons in the Music Theory section.

SECTION THREE

EAR TRAINING AND SIGHT SINGING

The student of sight singing learns to recognize the interval between any two successive notes and, upon seeing the notes on a page of music, is able to sing them. The student of ear training learns to recognize the interval between any two notes. He is able to sing any interval upon demand, and upon hearing an interval is able to identify it and write the notes—in any key he desires—on a sheet of manuscript paper. No matter whether one pursues the study of sight singing or ear training, one cannot learn one subject without, at the same time, becoming familiar with the other.

To SIGHT SING is to sing unfamiliar material upon reading it for the first time. When one becomes proficient at sight singing, it is as easy to sing the melody of an unfamiliar song as it is to read a newspaper.

The singer who has studied EAR TRAINING can listen to a song and at the same time write the notes on music manuscript paper.

Though the ability to sight sing is not essential, along with ear training, it is an important asset for anyone aspiring to sing on a professional level. For example, a knowledge of sight singing and ear training makes it easier to learn songs or harmony parts, and frees the singer from a dependence upon a musician to play the part on a musical instrument.

A fluent sight singer is able to read the music rather than depend solely upon memory during a performance. This is of particular value when providing vocal parts in the jingle and recording fields, and in background singing for film and TV.

TERMINOLOGY

SOLFEGE *(sole-FEZJ)* (French) *Note: ZJ is pronounced like the "s" in "pleasure."*

SOLFEGGIO *(sole-FEJ-ee-oh)* (Italian)

SOLFEGE, the French word, and **SOLFEGGIO**, the Italian equivalent, refer to the use of the syllables, Do, Re, Mi, etc., to name the tones of the scale when singing vocal exercises, melodies or harmonies.

SOLFEGE and **SOLFEGGIO** are frequently used as a synonym for sight singing.

On rare occasions, these words are intended to mean "the rudiments of music," or the performance of a vocal exercise on one vowel (the same as "vocalization").

SOLMIZATION *(sole-muh-ZAY-shun)* French spelling is *solmisation.*

SOLMIZATION is the act or system of using syllables such as Do, Re, Mi, to name the tones of the scale. This word has the same meaning as the first definition of SOLFEGE, above.

SYLLABLES which are used to name the tones of the scale begin with a consonant and end with the sound of a vowel.

SYSTEMS FOR SIGHT SINGING

The ideal sight singing system should be relatively easy to learn and simple to apply. The system that best meets these criteria is called the MOVABLE DO (pronounced *dough*) SYSTEM.

THE MOVABLE DO SYSTEM

In the Movable Do System, the syllable "Do" is always sung for the key note (tonic or 1st note) of the scale, no matter in which key the music is performed.

The 1st degree of the scale is sung with the syllable Do (pronounced *dough*).
The 2nd degree of the scale is sung with the syllable Re (pronounced *ray*).
The 3rd degree of the scale is sung with the syllable Mi (pronounced *mee*).
The 4th degree of the scale is sung with the syllable Fa (pronounced *fah*).
The 5th degree of the scale is sung with the syllable Sol (pronounced *so*).
The 6th degree of the scale is sung with the syllable La (pronounced *lah*).
The 7th degree of the scale is sung with the syllable Ti (pronounced *tee*).

The octave is Do, followed by the 9th degree of the scale which is Re, followed by the 10th degree of the scale which is Mi, etc.

The Movable Do System requires a constant awareness of the scale degree of each note of music being performed.

EXAMPLES

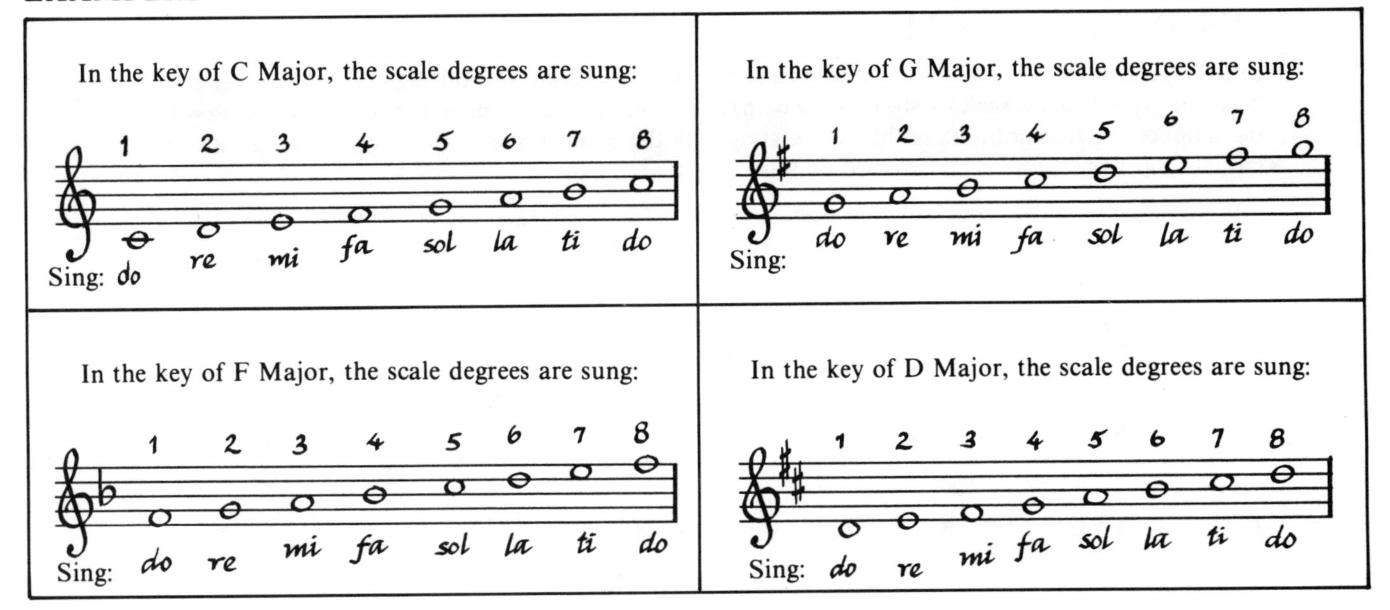

SHARPS AND FLATS

In the Movable Do System, sharps and flats are accommodated by additional syllables. For further information and for the pronunciation of the sharp and flat syllables, see pages 133 and 134.

TONIC SOL-FA *(TAH-nick sole-FAH)*

TONIC SOL-FA is another name for the movable do system.

THE STATIONARY DO SYSTEM (FIXED DO SYSTEM)

In the Stationary Do System

The note C is always sung with the syllable Do.
The note D is always sung with the syllable Re.
The note E is always sung with the syllable Mi.
The note F is always sung with the syllable Fa.
The note G is always sung with the syllable Sol.
The note A is always sung with the syllable La.
The note B is always sung with the syllable Si.

The syllable-note relationship remains the same regardless of the key in which the music is performed.

The Stationary Do System does not make any accommodation for sharps and flats. If, for example, the notes C, D, D# occur, they are sung Do, Re, Re. However, the second Re is sung one half step higher than the first Re.

SOL-FA *(sole-FAH)*

Do, Re, Mi, Fa, Sol, La, Ti (or Si)—which represent C, D, E, F, G, A, B—are called the sol-fa syllables. The use of these syllables is referred to as "sol-fa." The term "sol-fa" is usually used with reference to the stationary do system.

THE NUMBER SYSTEM

In the Number System, the degrees of the scale are numbered from one through seven. The key note (tonic or 1st note of the scale) is always sung with the number 1. The second note of the scale is sung with the number 2. The third note of the scale is sung with the number 3, etc. The octave is sung with the number 8 (or the number 1), followed by 9 (or 2), 10 (or 3), etc.

The Number System does not make any accommodation for sharps and flats. If, for example, in the Key of C Major, the notes C, D, D# occur, they are sung 1, 2, 2. However, the second 2 is sung one half step higher than the first 2.

The Number System is not ordinarily used by singers, but by musicians, who silently sing the numbers to themselves.

The number system loses the advantage of singable syllables and offers no other advantage in compensation.

THE LETTER SYSTEM (C, D, E, F, G, A, B)

In the Letter System, the letter names of the notes are sung.

The Letter System does not make any accommodations for sharps and flats. Also, it does not have the advantage of singable syllables. The Letter System is used very rarely.

THE SYLLABLE "LA" SYSTEM

In this system, the syllable "La" is used for all of the notes. As a result, the singer does not have to translate the pitch names into syllables. However, as in the Movable Do System, an awareness of the scale degree of each note is required.

DISADVANTAGES OF ALL FIXED DO SYSTEMS

The Stationary Do System and the Letter System are Fixed Do Systems. The disadvantage of all Fixed Do Systems is the progressive difficulty encountered as keys take on more sharps or flats. The Key of C is very easy; G and F are only a trifle harder; by the time the keys of three or four sharps or flats are reached, performance becomes extremely complex and very difficult. Movable Do Systems have, from the singer's point of view, only one key, and therefore are infinitely easier.

BEGINNING EAR TRAINING

The first three notes of the C Major scale are C, D, and E.

C is the first note of the C Major scale and is sung with the syllable Do.

D is the second note of the C Major scale and is sung with the syllable Re.

E is the third note of the C Major scale and is sung with the syllable Mi.

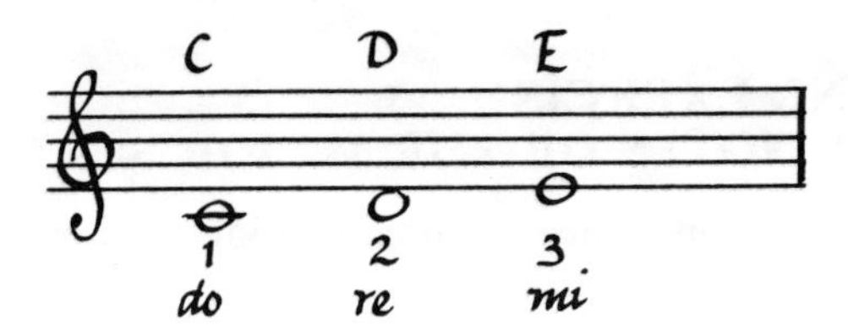

The interval from C to D is a MAJOR SECOND.
The interval from D to E is a MAJOR SECOND.
The interval from C to E is a MAJOR THIRD.

Because we are using a Movable Do System, any pitch can be used as a starting note for the following studies.

Each week's ear training assignment should be comprised of as many exercises as can be comfortably absorbed. Better too few exercises than too many.

FIRST EAR TRAINING EXERCISE
THE INTERVAL OF AN ASCENDING MAJOR SECOND

1. Using a musical instrument or pitch pipe, randomly produce a tone.
2. Listen carefully to the tone you have produced and fix it in your mind.
3. Using the syllable Do, sing the tone.
4. Using the syllable Re, sing a note that is a Major Second higher. As a learning aid, think of the first two notes of *Oh, Susanna* or *Frankie and Johnnie* or *Polly Wolly Doodle* or *Alouette* or *Bill Bailey*.
5. Repeat this exercise many times, using randomly selected pitches.

SECOND EAR TRAINING EXERCISE
THE INTERVAL OF AN ASCENDING MAJOR THIRD

1. Using a musical instrument or pitch pipe, randomly produce a tone.
2. Listen carefully to the tone you have produced and fix it in your mind.
3. Using the syllable Do, sing the tone.
4. Using the syllable Mi, sing a note that is a Major Third higher. As a learning aid, think of the first two notes of *The Marines' Hymn* or *Michael, Row the Boat Ashore.*
5. Repeat this exercise many times using randomly selected pitches.

THIRD EAR TRAINING EXERCISE
THE INTERVAL OF A DESCENDING MAJOR SECOND

1. Using a musical instrument or pitch pipe, randomly produce a tone.
2. Listen carefully to the tone you have produced and fix it in your mind.
3. Using the syllable Re, sing the tone.
4. Using the syllable Do, sing a note that is a Major Second lower. As a learning aid, think of the first two notes of *Satin Doll* or *Yesterday* or *Alfie* or *Love Is Blue.*
5. Repeat this exercise many times using randomly selected pitches.

FOURTH EAR TRAINING EXERCISE
THE INTERVAL OF A DESCENDING MAJOR THIRD

1. Using a musical instrument or pitch pipe, randomly produce a tone.
2. Listen carefully to the tone you have produced and fix it in your mind.
3. Using the syllable Mi, sing the tone.
4. Using the syllable Do, sing a note that is a Major Third lower. As a learning aid, think of the first interval of *Skip to My Lou* or *Swing Low, Sweet Chariot.*
5. Repeat this exercise many times using randomly selected pitches.

FIFTH EAR TRAINING EXERCISE
THE FIRST THREE NOTES OF THE MAJOR SCALE—ASCENDING

1. Using a musical instrument or pitch pipe, randomly produce a tone.
2. Listen carefully to the tone you have produced and fix it in your mind.
3. Using the syllable Do, sing the tone.
4. Sing the first three notes of the Major scale, using the syllables Do, Re, Mi. As a learning aid, think of the first three notes of *Oh, Susanna* or *Frankie and Johnnie* or *Polly Wolly Doodle* or *Alouette.*
5. Repeat this exercise many times using randomly selected pitches.

SIXTH EAR TRAINING EXERCISE
THE FIRST THREE NOTES OF THE MAJOR SCALE—DESCENDING

1. Using a musical instrument or pitch pipe, randomly produce a tone.
2. Listen carefully to the tone you have produced and fix it in your mind.
3. Using the syllable Mi, sing the tone.
4. In descending order, sing the first three notes of the Major scale, using the syllables Mi, Re, Do. As a learning aid, think of the first three notes of *Three Blind Mice* or *Merrily We Roll Along* or *Old Folks at Home (Way Down Upon the Swanee River).*
5. Repeat this exercise many times using randomly selected pitches.

LEARNING TO SIGHT SING IN THE KEY OF C MAJOR

As we have learned, the first three notes of the C Major scale are C, D, and E, and these three notes are sung respectively with the syllables Do, Re, and Mi.

The first twelve sight singing exercises contain only the notes C, D, and E. Because we are using a Movable Do System, any pitch can be used as a starting note for the following studies.

Each exercise is to be sung at least twice each day. The first time, the scale degree number (1, 2, 3) is to be sung. The second time, the syllable (Do, Re, Mi) is to be sung.

Each week's sight singing lesson assignment should be comprised of as many exercises as can be comfortably absorbed. Better too few exercises than too many.

Do not play any exercise on a musical instrument before first singing it. When necessary, a musical instrument or a pitch pipe may be used to check for accuracy.

When singing an interval which is not yet fixed in your mind, think of the scale and the degrees through which you must pass until reaching the desired note. For example, when attempting the interval of Do to Mi, think of the note Re, through which you must pass.

Before singing an exercise, read it through silently, thinking first of the number name and sound, next of the syllable name and sound.

Take a breath whenever it is comfortable to do so, the same as when speaking. All of the sight singing exercises are to be sung legato.

SIGHT SINGING EXERCISES 1 THROUGH 12

EAR TRAINING—THE FIRST FOUR NOTES OF THE MAJOR SCALE

The first four notes of the C Major scale are C, D, E, and F.

C, D, and E are the first three notes of the C Major scale, and are sung with the syllables Do, Re, and Mi.

F is the fourth note of the C Major scale, and is sung with the syllable Fa.

The interval from C to D is a MAJOR SECOND.
The interval from D to E is a MAJOR SECOND.
The interval from E to F is a MINOR SECOND.
The interval from C to E is a MAJOR THIRD.
The interval from D to F is a MINOR THIRD.
The interval from C to F is a PERFECT FOURTH.

Because we are using a Movable Do System, any pitch can be used as a starting note for the following studies.

Each week's ear training assignment should be comprised of as many exercises as can be comfortably absorbed. Better too few exercises than too many.

SEVENTH EAR TRAINING EXERCISE
THE INTERVAL OF AN ASCENDING MINOR SECOND

1. Using a musical instrument or pitch pipe, randomly produce a tone.
2. Listen carefully to the tone you have produced and fix it in your mind.
3. Using the syllable Mi, sing the tone.
4. Using the syllable Fa, sing a note that is a Minor Second higher. As a learning aid, think of the first two notes of *As Time Goes By* or *I'm In the Mood for Love* or *But Beautiful* or *By the Time I Get to Phoenix* or *By the Light of the Silvery Moon.*
5. Repeat this exercise many times using randomly selected pitches.

EIGHTH EAR TRAINING EXERCISE
THE INTERVAL OF A DESCENDING MINOR SECOND

1. Using a musical instrument or pitch pipe, randomly produce a tone.
2. Listen carefully to the tone you have produced and fix it in your mind.
3. Using the syllable Fa, sing the tone.
4. Using the syllable Mi, sing a note that is a Minor Second lower. As a learning aid, think of the first two notes of *Fly Me to the Moon* or *April Showers* or *Oh, Babe, What Would You Say* or *Some Enchanted Evening* or *Cuddle Up a Little Closer.*
5. Repeat this exercise many times using randomly selected pitches.

NINTH EAR TRAINING EXERCISE
THE INTERVAL OF AN ASCENDING MINOR THIRD

1. Using a musical instrument or pitch pipe, randomly produce a tone.
2. Listen carefully to the tone you have produced and fix it in your mind.
3. Using the syllable Re, sing the tone.
4. Using the syllable Fa, sing a note that is a Minor Third higher. As a learning aid, think of the first two notes of *Don't Blame Me* or *On a Clear Day* or *Close to You* or *What the World Needs Now Is Love* or *Hello, Dolly* or *Georgia On My Mind* or *The Very Thought of You* or the first interval of *Foggy Day.*
5. Repeat this exercise many times using randomly selected pitches.

TENTH EAR TRAINING EXERCISE
THE INTERVAL OF A DESCENDING MINOR THIRD

1. Using a musical instrument or pitch pipe, randomly produce a tone.
2. Listen carefully to the tone you have produced and fix it in your mind.
3. Using the syllable Fa, sing the tone.
4. Using the syllable Re, sing a note that is a Minor Third lower. As a learning aid, think of the first two notes of *When Irish Eyes Are Smiling* or *Didn't We* or *The Girl from Ipanema* or *Misty* or *Tea for Two* or *Zing Went the Strings of My Heart.*
5. Repeat this exercise many times using randomly selected pitches.

ELEVENTH EAR TRAINING EXERCISE
THE INTERVAL OF AN ASCENDING PERFECT FOURTH

1. Using a musical instrument or pitch pipe, randomly produce a tone.
2. Listen carefully to the tone you have produced and fix it in your mind.
3. Using the syllable Do, sing the tone.
4. Using the syllable Fa, sing a note that is a Perfect Fourth higher. As a learning aid, think of the first two notes of *Here Comes the Bride* or *Auld Lang Syne* or *Because* or *Never On Sunday* or *Matchmaker* or *Sunrise, Sunset.*
5. Repeat this exercise many times using randomly selected pitches.

TWELFTH EAR TRAINING EXERCISE
THE INTERVAL OF A DESCENDING PERFECT FOURTH

1. Using a musical instrument or pitch pipe, randomly produce a tone.
2. Listen carefully to the tone you have produced and fix it in your mind.
3. Using the syllable Fa, sing the tone.
4. Using the syllable Do, sing a note that is a Perfect Fourth lower. As a learning aid, think of the first two notes of *Born Free* or *Softly, as In a Morning Sunrise* or *King of the Road* or *Yes, We Have No Bananas* or the first interval of *Clementine.*
5. Repeat this exercise many times using randomly selected pitches.

SIGHT SINGING—THE FIRST FOUR NOTES OF THE MAJOR SCALE

The first four notes of the C Major scale are C, D, E, and F. These four notes are sung with the syllables Do, Re, Mi, and Fa.

Sight singing exercises Thirteen through Twenty-Three contain only the notes C, D, E, and F. Because we are using a Movable Do System, any pitch can be used as a starting note for the following studies.

Each exercise is to be sung at least twice each day. The first time, the scale degree number (1, 2, 3, 4) is to be sung. The second time, the syllable (Do, Re, Mi, Fa) is to be sung.

Each week's sight singing lesson assignment should be comprised of as many exercises as can be comfortably absorbed. Better too few exercises than too many.

Do not play any exercise on a musical instrument before first singing it. When necessary, a musical instrument or a pitch pipe may be used to check for accuracy.

When singing an interval which is not yet fixed in your mind, think of the scale and the degrees through which you must pass until reaching the desired note. For example, when attempting the interval of Do to Fa, think of the notes Re and Mi, through which you must pass.

Before singing an exercise, read it through silently, thinking first of the number name and sound, next of the syllable name and sound.

Take a breath whenever it is comfortable to do so, the same as when speaking. All of the sight singing exercises are to be sung legato.

SIGHT SINGING EXERCISES 13 THROUGH 23

EAR TRAINING—THE FIRST FIVE NOTES OF THE MAJOR SCALE

The first five notes of the C Major scale are C, D, E, F, and G.

C, D, E, and F are the first four notes of the C Major scale, and are sung with the syllables Do, Re, Mi and Fa.

G is the fifth note of the C Major scale, and is sung with the syllable Sol, which is pronounced "So."

The interval from C to D is a MAJOR SECOND.
The interval from D to E is a MAJOR SECOND.
The interval from E to F is a MINOR SECOND.
The interval from F to G is a MAJOR SECOND.
The interval from C to E is a MAJOR THIRD.
The interval from D to F is a MINOR THIRD.
The interval from E to G is a MINOR THIRD.
The interval from C to F is a PERFECT FOURTH.
The interval from D to G is a PERFECT FOURTH.
The interval from C to G is a PERFECT FIFTH.

Because we are using a Movable Do System, any pitch can be used as a starting note for the following studies.

Each week's ear training assignment should be comprised of as many exercises as can be comfortably absorbed. Better too few exercises than too many.

THIRTEENTH EAR TRAINING EXERCISE
THE INTERVAL OF AN ASCENDING PERFECT FIFTH

1. Using a musical instrument or pitch pipe, randomly produce a tone.
2. Listen carefully to the tone you have produced and fix it in your mind.
3. Using the syllable Do, sing the tone.
4. Using the syllable Sol, sing a note that is a Perfect Fifth higher. As a learning aid, think of the first two notes of *People Will Say We're In Love* or *Georgy Girl* or *It Ain't Necessarily So* or *Two Sleepy People* or *I Cried for You* or *Summer of '42 Theme* or *Moon River* or the first interval of *Twinkle, Twinkle, Little Star.*
5. Repeat this exercise many times using randomly selected pitches.

FOURTEENTH EAR TRAINING EXERCISE
THE INTERVAL OF A DESCENDING PERFECT FIFTH

1. Using a musical instrument or pitch pipe, randomly produce a tone.
2. Listen carefully to the tone you have produced and fix it in your mind.
3. Using the syllable Sol, sing the tone.
4. Using the syllable Do, sing a note that is a Perfect Fifth lower. As a learning aid, think of the first two notes of *Feelings* or *Easy to Love* or *The Way You Look Tonight.*
5. Repeat this exercise many times using randomly selected pitches.

SIGHT SINGING—THE FIRST FIVE NOTES OF THE MAJOR SCALE

The first five notes of the C Major scale are C, D, E, F, and G. These five notes are sung with the syllables Do, Re, Mi, Fa, and Sol.

Sight singing exercises Twenty-Four through Thirty-Four contain only the notes C, D, E, F, and G. Because we are using a Movable Do System, any pitch can be used as a starting note for the following studies.

Each exercise is to be sung at least twice each day. The first time, the scale degree number (1, 2, 3, 4, 5) is to be sung. The second time, the syllable (Do, Re, Mi, Fa, Sol) is to be sung.

Each week's sight singing assignment should be comprised of as many exercises as can be comfortably absorbed. Better too few exercises than too many.

Do not play any exercise on a musical instrument before first singing it. When necessary a musical instrument or a pitch pipe may be used to check for accuracy.

When singing an interval which is not yet fixed in your mind, think of the scale and the degrees through which you must pass until reaching the desired note. For example, when attempting the interval of Do to Sol, think of the notes Re, Mi, and Fa, through which you must pass.

Before singing an exercise, read it through silently, thinking first of the number name and sound, next of the syllable name and sound.

Take a breath whenever it is comfortable to do so, the same as when speaking. All of the sight singing exercises are to be sung legato.

THE ARPEGGIO *(are-PEJ-ee-oh)*

ARPEGGIO means "harplike." An arpeggio is produced by singing the notes of a chord in succession. The arpeggio is also referred to as a "broken chord." An arpeggio may be sung from the lowest note of the chord to the highest, or from the highest note to the lowest. At times the notes of the arpeggio are sung out of sequence. The three notes of a Major chord arpeggio (Do, Mi, Sol) appear in Exercise Twenty-Six. To recall quickly the sound of the ascending Major chord arpeggio, think of the first three notes of *The Marines' Hymn* or *Michael, Row the Boat Ashore.* It is very important for the student to become familiar with the sound of the ascending and descending Major chord arpeggio.

SIGHT SINGING EXERCISES 24 THROUGH 34

EAR TRAINING—A ONE OCTAVE MAJOR SCALE

The eight notes of a one octave C Major scale are C, D, E, F, G, A, B, and C.

C, D, E, F, and G are the first five notes of the C Major scale, and are sung with the syllables Do, Re, Mi, Fa, and Sol.

A is the sixth note of the C Major scale, and is sung with the syllable La. B is the seventh note of the C Major scale, and is sung with the syllable Ti. C is the octave (eighth note) of the C Major scale, and is sung with the syllable Do. The number 1 is sung for the first degree and the eighth degree of the scale.

The interval from C to D is a MAJOR SECOND.
The interval from D to E is a MAJOR SECOND.
The interval from F to G is a MAJOR SECOND.
The interval from G to A is a MAJOR SECOND.
The interval from A to B is a MAJOR SECOND.
The interval from E to F is a MINOR SECOND.
The interval from B to C is a MINOR SECOND.
The interval from C to E is a MAJOR THIRD.
The interval from F to A is a MAJOR THIRD.
The interval from G to B is a MAJOR THIRD.
The interval from D to F is a MINOR THIRD.
The interval from E to G is a MINOR THIRD.
The interval from A to C is a MINOR THIRD.
The interval from C to F is a PERFECT FOURTH.
The interval from D to G is a PERFECT FOURTH.
The interval from E to A is a PERFECT FOURTH.
The interval from G to C is a PERFECT FOURTH.
The interval from F to B is an AUGMENTED FOURTH.
The interval from C to G is a PERFECT FIFTH.
The interval from D to A is a PERFECT FIFTH.
The interval from E to B is a PERFECT FIFTH.
The interval from F to C is a PERFECT FIFTH.
The interval from C to A is a MAJOR SIXTH.
The interval from D to B is a MAJOR SIXTH.
The interval from E to C is a MINOR SIXTH.
The interval from C to B is a MAJOR SEVENTH.
The interval from D to C is a MINOR SEVENTH.
The interval from C to C is a PERFECT OCTAVE.

Because we are using a Movable Do System, any pitch can be used as a starting note for the following studies.

Each week's ear training assignment should be comprised of as many exercises as can be comfortably absorbed. Better too few exercises than too many.

FIFTEENTH EAR TRAINING EXERCISE
THE INTERVAL OF AN ASCENDING AUGMENTED FOURTH

1. Using a musical instrument or pitch pipe, randomly produce a tone.
2. Listen carefully to the tone you have produced and fix it in your mind.
3. Using the syllable Fa, sing the tone.
4. Using the syllable Ti, sing a note that is an Augmented Fourth higher. To help learn this difficult interval, it should be played repeatedly on a musical instrument or pitch pipe.
5. Repeat this exercise many times using randomly selected pitches.

SIXTEENTH EAR TRAINING EXERCISE
THE INTERVAL OF A DESCENDING AUGMENTED FOURTH

1. Using a musical instrument or pitch pipe, randomly produce a tone.
2. Listen carefully to the tone you have produced and fix it in your mind.
3. Using the syllable Ti, sing the tone.
4. Using the syllable Fa, sing a note that is an Augmented Fourth lower. To help learn this difficult interval it should be played repeatedly on a musical instrument or pitch pipe.
5. Repeat this exercise many times using randomly selected pitches.

SEVENTEENTH EAR TRAINING EXERCISE
THE INTERVAL OF AN ASCENDING MAJOR SIXTH

1. Using a musical instrument or pitch pipe, randomly produce a tone.
2. Listen carefully to the tone you have produced and fix it in your mind.
3. Using the syllable Do, sing the tone.
4. Using the syllable La, sing a note that is a Major Sixth higher. As a learning aid, think of the first two notes of *My Bonnie Lies Over the Ocean* or *My Wild Irish Rose* or *To Each His Own* or *My Way* or *Beyond the Blue Horizon* or *A Fellow Needs a Girl* or *Days of Wine and Roses.*
5. Repeat this exercise many times using randomly selected pitches.

EIGHTEENTH EAR TRAINING EXERCISE
THE INTERVAL OF A DESCENDING MAJOR SIXTH

1. Using a musical instrument or pitch pipe, randomly produce a tone.
2. Listen carefully to the tone you have produced and fix it in your mind.
3. Using the syllable La, sing the tone.
4. Using the syllable Do, sing a note that is a Major Sixth lower. As a learning aid, think of the first two notes of *Over There* or *Bye, Bye, Blues.*
5. Repeat this exercise many times using randomly selected pitches.

NINETEENTH EAR TRAINING EXERCISE
THE INTERVAL OF AN ASCENDING MINOR SIXTH

1. Using a musical instrument or pitch pipe, randomly produce a tone.
2. Listen carefully to the tone you have produced and fix it in your mind.
3. Using the syllable Mi, sing the tone.
4. Using the syllable Do, sing a note that is a Minor Sixth higher. As a learning aid, think of the first two notes of *A Day In the Life of a Fool.* If this melody is unfamiliar, think of a note that is a Major Sixth higher, then lower that note a Minor Second.
5. Repeat this exercise many times using randomly selected pitches.

TWENTIETH EAR TRAINING EXERCISE
THE INTERVAL OF A DESCENDING MINOR SIXTH

1. Using a musical instrument or pitch pipe, randomly produce a tone.
2. Listen carefully to the tone you have produced and fix it in your mind.
3. Using the syllable Do, sing the tone.
4. Using the syllable Mi, sing a note that is a Minor Sixth lower. As a learning aid, think of the first two notes of *All My Love* or *Where Do I Begin (Love Story).*
5. Repeat this exercise many times using randomly selected pitches.

TWENTY-FIRST EAR TRAINING EXERCISE
THE INTERVAL OF AN ASCENDING PERFECT OCTAVE

1. Using a musical instrument or pitch pipe, randomly produce a tone.
2. Listen carefully to the tone you have produced and fix it in your mind.
3. Using the syllable Do, sing the tone.
4. Using the syllable Do, sing a note that is a Perfect Octave higher. As a learning aid, think of the first two notes of *Bali Ha'i* or *When You Wish Upon a Star* or *I Wonder What's Become of Sally* or *Somewhere Over the Rainbow.*
5. Repeat this exercise many times using randomly selected pitches.

TWENTY-SECOND EAR TRAINING EXERCISE
THE INTERVAL OF A DESCENDING PERFECT OCTAVE

1. Using a musical instrument or pitch pipe, randomly produce a tone.
2. Listen carefully to the tone you have produced and fix it in your mind.
3. Using the syllable Do, sing the tone.
4. Using the syllable Do, sing a note that is a Perfect Octave lower. As a learning aid, think of the first two notes of *Willow, Weep for Me* or *Love Is Sweeping the Country.*
5. Repeat this exercise many times using randomly selected pitches.

TWENTY-THIRD EAR TRAINING EXERCISE
THE INTERVAL OF AN ASCENDING MAJOR SEVENTH

1. Using a musical instrument or pitch pipe, randomly produce a tone.
2. Listen carefully to the tone you have produced and fix it in your mind.
3. Using the syllable Do, sing the tone.
4. Using the syllable Ti, sing a note that is a Major Seventh higher. As a learning aid, think of a note that is a Perfect Octave higher, then lower that note a Minor Second.
5. Repeat this exercise many times using randomly selected pitches.

TWENTY-FOURTH EAR TRAINING EXERCISE
THE INTERVAL OF A DESCENDING MAJOR SEVENTH

1. Using a musical instrument or pitch pipe, randomly produce a tone.
2. Listen carefully to the tone you have produced and fix it in your mind.
3. Using the syllable Ti, sing the tone.
4. Using the syllable Do, sing a note that is a Major Seventh lower. As a learning aid, think of a note that is a Perfect Octave lower, then raise that note a Minor Second.
5. Repeat this exercise many times using randomly selected pitches.

TWENTY-FIFTH EAR TRAINING EXERCISE
THE INTERVAL OF AN ASCENDING MINOR SEVENTH

1. Using a musical instrument or pitch pipe, randomly produce a tone.
2. Listen carefully to the tone you have produced and fix it in your mind.
3. Using the syllable Re, sing the tone.
4. Using the syllable Do, sing a note that is a Minor Seventh higher. As a learning aid, think of the first two notes of *Somewhere* (from *West Side Story).* If this melody is unfamiliar, think of a note that is a Perfect Octave higher, then lower that note a Major Second.
5. Repeat this exercise many times using randomly selected pitches.

TWENTY-SIXTH EAR TRAINING EXERCISE
THE INTERVAL OF A DESCENDING MINOR SEVENTH

1. Using a musical instrument or pitch pipe, randomly produce a tone.
2. Listen carefully to the tone you have produced and fix it in your mind.
3. Using the syllable Do, sing the tone.
4. Using the syllable Re, sing a note that is a Minor Seventh lower. As a learning aid, think of a note that is a Perfect Octave lower, then raise that note a Major Second.
5. Repeat this exercise many times using randomly selected pitches.

THIS CONCLUDES THE EAR TRAINING EXERCISES. THE STUDENT IS TO CONTINUALLY REVIEW ALL OF THE PRECEDING EAR TRAINING EXERCISES.

SIGHT SINGING—A ONE OCTAVE MAJOR SCALE

The eight notes of a one octave C Major scale are C, D, E, F, G, A, B, and C. These eight notes are sung with the syllables Do, Re, Mi, Fa, Sol, La, Ti, and Do.

When performing the sight singing studies, the throat is to be relaxed. Sing softly and without strain. If notes should occur which are too high or too low to be comfortably accommodated by the vocal range, the student is to "think" the notes (sing the notes in the mind) rather than sing the notes aloud. If convenient, the student may lower or raise troublesome passages an octave to bring them within the vocal range.

Exercises Thirty-Five through Forty-Five contain the notes C, D, E, F, G, A, B, and C (the notes comprising a one octave C Major Scale). Because we are using a Movable Do System, you may begin singing with any pitch that feels comfortable.

Each exercise is to be sung at least twice each day. The first time, the scale degree number (1, 2, 3, 4, 5, 6, 7, 1) is to be sung. The second time, the syllable (Do, Re, Mi, Fa, Sol, La, Ti, Do) is to be sung.

Each week's lesson should be comprised of as many exercises as can be comfortably absorbed. Better too few exercises than too many.

Do not play any exercise on a musical instrument before first singing it. When necessary, a musical instrument or a pitch pipe may be used to check for accuracy.

Take a breath whenever it is comfortable to do so. All of the sight singing exercises are to be sung legato.

Think the sound of each note before you sing it.

SIGHT SINGING EXERCISE 35 THROUGH 45

THREE MORE NOTES—KEY OF C MAJOR

Three more notes included in the studies that follow are G (5—Sol), A (6—La), B (7—Ti).

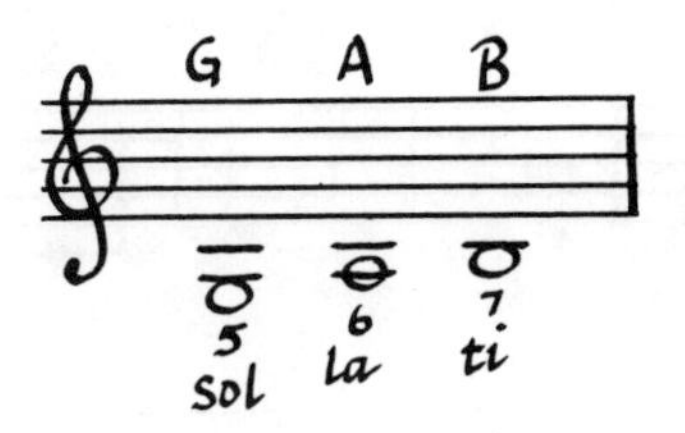

ALL OF THE NOTES WE HAVE LEARNED

When performing the sight singing studies, the throat is to be relaxed. Sing softly and without strain. If notes should occur which are too high or too low to be comfortably accommodated by the vocal range, the student is to "think" the notes (sing the notes in the mind) rather than sing the notes aloud. If convenient, the student may lower or raise troublesome passages an octave to bring them within the vocal range.

Exercises Forty-Six through Fifty-Six contain the notes comprising the extended C Major Scale. Because we are using a Movable Do System, you may begin singing with any pitch that feels comfortable.

Each exercise is to be sung at least twice each day. The first time, the scale degree number (1, 2, 3, 4, 5, 6, 7) is to be sung. The second time, the syllable (Do, Re, Mi, Fa, Sol, La, Ti) is to be sung.

Each week's lesson should be comprised of as many exercises as can be comfortably absorbed.

Do not play any exercise on a musical instrument before singing it. When necessary, a musical instrument or a pitch pipe may be used to check for accuracy.

Take a breath whenever it is comfortable to do so. All of the sight singing exercises are to be sung legato.

Think the sound of each note before you sing it.

SIGHT SINGING EXERCISES 46 THROUGH 56

FIVE MORE NOTES—KEY OF C MAJOR

Five more notes included in the studies that follow are D (2—Re), E (3—Mi), F (4—Fa), G (5—Sol), A (6—La).

ALL OF THE NOTES WE HAVE LEARNED

When performing the sight singing studies, the throat is to be relaxed. Sing softly and without strain. If notes should occur which are too high or too low to be comfortably accommodated by the vocal range, the student is to "think" the notes (sing the notes in the mind) rather than sing the notes aloud. If convenient, the student may lower or raise troublesome passages an octave to bring them within the vocal range.

Exercises Fifty-Seven through Sixty-Seven contain all the notes we have learned. Because we are using a Movable Do System, you may begin singing with any pitch that feels comfortable.

Each exercise is to be sung at least twice each day. The first time, the scale degree number (1, 2, 3, 4, 5, 6, 7) is to be sung. The second time, the syllable (Do, Re, Mi, Fa, Sol, La, Ti) is to be sung.

Each week's lesson should be comprised of as many exercises as can be comfortably absorbed.

Do not play any exercise on a musical instrument before first singing it. When necessary, a musical instrument or a pitch pipe may be used to check for accuracy.

Take a breath whenever it is comfortable to do so. All of the sight singing exercises are to be sung legato.

Think the sound of each note before you sing it.

SIGHT SINGING EXERCISES 57 THROUGH 67

LET'S LEARN TO SIGHT SING IN THE KEY OF G MAJOR

SIGHT SINGING THE FIRST THREE NOTES OF THE G MAJOR SCALE

The first three notes of the G Major scale are G, A, and B.

G is the first note of the G Major scale, and is sung with the syllable Do.

A is the second note of the G Major scale, and is sung with the syllable Re.

B is the third note of the G Major scale, and is sung with the syllable Mi.

The interval from G (the first degree of the scale) to A (the second degree of the scale) is a MAJOR SECOND.

The interval from G (the first degree of the scale) to B (the third degree of the scale) is a MAJOR THIRD.

The interval from A (the second degree of the scale) to B (the third degree of the scale) is a MAJOR SECOND.

Exercises Sixty-Eight through Seventy-Eight contain only the notes G, A, and B. Because we are using a Movable Do System, you may begin singing with any pitch that feels comfortable.

Each exercise is to be sung at least twice each day. The first time, the scale degree number (1, 2, 3) is to be sung. The second time, the syllable (Do, Re, Mi) is to be sung.

Each week's sight singing lesson assignment should be comprised of as many exercises as can be comfortably absorbed. Better too few exercises than too many.

Do not play any exercise on a musical instrument before first singing it. When necessary, a musical instrument or a pitch pipe may be used to check for accuracy.

When singing an interval which is not yet fixed in your mind, think of the scale and the degrees through which you must pass until reaching the desired note.

Before singing an exercise, read it through silently, thinking first of the number name and sound, next of the syllable name and sound.

Take a breath whenever it is comfortable to do so, the same as when speaking. All of the sight singing exercises are to be sung legato.

SIGHT SINGING EXERCISES 68 THROUGH 78

SIGHT SINGING THE FIRST FOUR NOTES OF THE G MAJOR SCALE

The first four notes of the G Major scale are G, A, B, and C.

G, A, and B are the first three notes of the G Major scale, and are sung with the syllables Do, Re, and Mi.

C is the fourth note of the G Major scale, and is sung with the syllable Fa.

The interval from G to A is a MAJOR SECOND.
The interval from A to B is a MAJOR SECOND.
The interval from B to C is a MINOR SECOND.
The interval from G to B is a MAJOR THIRD.
The interval from A to C is a MINOR THIRD.
The interval from G to C is a PERFECT FOURTH.

Exercises Seventy-Nine through Eighty-Nine contain the notes G, A, B, and C. Because we are using a Movable Do System, you may begin singing with any pitch that feels comfortable.

Each exercise is to be sung at least twice each day. The first time, the scale degree number (1, 2, 3, 4) is to be sung. The second time, the syllable (Do, Re, Mi, Fa) is to be sung.

Each week's lesson should be comprised of as many exercises as can be comfortably absorbed.

Do not play any exercise on a musical instrument before first singing it. When necessary, a musical instrument or a pitch pipe may be used to check for accuracy.

Take a breath whenever it is comfortable to do so. All of the sight singing exercises are to be sung legato.

Think the sound of each note before you sing it.

SIGHT SINGING EXERCISES 79 THROUGH 89

SIGHT SINGING THE FIRST FIVE NOTES OF THE G MAJOR SCALE

The first five notes of the G Major scale are G, A, B, C, and D.

G, A, B, and C are the first four notes of the G Major scale, and are sung with the syllables Do, Re, Mi, and Fa.

D is the fifth note of the G Major scale, and is sung with the syllable Sol.

The interval from G to A is a MAJOR SECOND.
The interval from A to B is a MAJOR SECOND.
The interval from C to D is a MAJOR SECOND.
The interval from B to C is a MINOR SECOND.
The interval from G to B is a MAJOR THIRD.
The interval from A to C is a MINOR THIRD.
The interval from B to D is a MINOR THIRD.
The interval from G to C is a PERFECT FOURTH.
The interval from A to D is a PERFECT FOURTH.
The interval from G to D is a PERFECT FIFTH.

A Major chord arpeggio (Do, Mi, Sol) appears in Exercises Ninety-Three, Ninety-Five, and Ninety-Nine. To recall quickly the sound of the ascending Major Chord arpeggio, think of the first three notes of the song *The Marines' Hymn* or *Michael, Row the Boat Ashore.*

Exercises Ninety through One Hundred contain the notes G, A, B, C, and D. Because we are using a Movable Do System, you may begin singing with any pitch that feels comfortable.

Each exercise is to be sung at least twice each day. The first time, the scale degree number (1, 2, 3, 4, 5) is to be sung. The second time, the syllable (Do, Re, Mi, Fa, Sol) is to be sung.

Each week's lesson should be comprised of as many exercises as can be comfortably absorbed.

Do not play any exercise on a musical instrument before first singing it. When necessary, a musical instrument or a pitch pipe may be used to check for accuracy.

Take a breath whenever it is comfortable to do so. All of the sight singing exercises are to be sung legato.

Think the sound of each note before you sing it.

SIGHT SINGING EXERCISES 90 THROUGH 100

SINGING A ONE OCTAVE G MAJOR SCALE

The eight notes of a one octave G Major scale are G, A, B, C, D, E, F#, and G.

G, A, B, C, and D are the first five notes of the G Major scale, and are sung with the syllables Do, Re, Mi, Fa, and Sol.

E is the sixth note of the G Major scale, and is sung with the syllable La. F# is the seventh note of the G Major scale, and is sung with the syllable Ti. G is the octave (eighth note) of the G Major scale, and is sung with the syllable Do. The number 1 is sung for the first degree and the eighth degree of the scale.

The interval from G to A is a MAJOR SECOND.
The interval from A to B is a MAJOR SECOND.
The interval from C to D is a MAJOR SECOND.
The interval from D to E is a MAJOR SECOND.
The interval from E to F# is a MAJOR SECOND.
The interval from B to C is a MINOR SECOND.
The interval from F# to G is a MINOR SECOND.
The interval from G to B is a MAJOR THIRD.
The interval from C to E is a MAJOR THIRD.
The interval from D to F# is a MAJOR THIRD.
The interval from A to C is a MINOR THIRD.
The interval from B to D is a MINOR THIRD.
The interval from E to G is a MINOR THIRD.
The interval from G to C is a PERFECT FOURTH.
The interval from A to D is a PERFECT FOURTH.
The interval from B to E is a PERFECT FOURTH.
The interval from D to G is a PERFECT FOURTH.
The interval from C to F# is an AUGMENTED FOURTH.
The interval from G to D is a PERFECT FIFTH.
The interval from A to E is a PERFECT FIFTH.
The interval from B to F# is a PERFECT FIFTH.
The interval from C to G is a PERFECT FIFTH.
The interval from G to E is a MAJOR SIXTH.
The interval from A to F# is a MAJOR SIXTH.
The interval from B to G is a MINOR SIXTH.
The interval from G to F# is a MAJOR SEVENTH.
The interval from A to G is a MINOR SEVENTH.
The interval from G to G is a PERFECT OCTAVE.

Exercises One Hundred One through One Hundred Eleven contain the notes G, A, B, C, D, E, F#, and G (the notes comprising a one octave G Major scale). Because we are using a Movable Do System, you may begin singing with any pitch that feels comfortable.

Each exercise is to be sung at least twice each day. The first time, the scale degree number (1, 2, 3, 4, 5, 6, 7, 1) is to be sung. The second time, the syllable (Do, Re, Mi, Fa, Sol, La, Ti, Do) is to be sung.

Each week's lesson should be comprised of as many exercises as can be comfortably absorbed.

Do not play any exercise on a musical instrument before first singing it. When necessary, a musical instrument or a pitch pipe may be used to check for accuracy.

Take a breath whenever it is comfortable to do so. All of the sight singing exercises are to be sung legato.

Think the sound of each note before you sing it.

If notes should occur which are too high or too low to be comfortably accommodated by the vocal range, the student is to "think" the notes (sing the notes in the mind) rather than sing the notes aloud. If convenient, the student may lower or raise troublesome passages an octave to bring them within the vocal range.

SIGHT SINGING EXERCISES 101 THROUGH 111

THREE MORE NOTES—KEY OF G MAJOR

Three more notes included in the studies that follow are D (5—Sol), E (6—La), F# (7—Ti).

ALL THE NOTES WE HAVE LEARNED

When performing the sight singing studies, the throat is to be relaxed. Sing softly and without strain. If notes should occur which are too high or too low to be comfortably accommodated by the vocal range, the student is to "think" the notes (sing the notes in the mind) rather than sing the notes aloud. If convenient, the student may lower or raise troublesome passages an octave to bring them within the vocal range.

Exercises One Hundred Twelve through One Hundred Twenty-Two contain the notes comprising the extended G Major scale. Because we are using a Movable Do System, you may begin singing with any pitch that feels comfortable.

Each exercise is to be sung at least twice each day. The first time, the scale degree number (1, 2, 3, 4, 5, 6, 7) is to be sung. The second time, the syllable (Do, Re, Mi, Fa, Sol, La, Ti) is to be sung.

Each week's lesson should be comprised of as many exercises as can be comfortably absorbed.

Do not play any exercise on a musical instrument before first singing it. When necessary, a musical instrument or a pitch pipe may be used to check for accuracy.

Take a breath whenever it is comfortable to do so. All of the sight singing exercises are to be sung legato.

Think the sound of each note before you sing it.

SIGHT SINGING EXERCISES 112 THROUGH 122

TWO MORE NOTES—KEY OF G MAJOR

Two more notes included in the studies that follow are C (4—Fa) and A (2—Re).

ALL OF THE NOTES WE HAVE LEARNED

When performing the sight singing studies, the throat is to be relaxed. Sing softly and without strain. If notes should occur which are too high or too low to be comfortably accommodated by the vocal range, the student is to "think" the notes (sing the notes in the mind) rather than sing the notes aloud. If convenient, the student may lower or raise troublesome passages an octave to bring them within the vocal range.

Exercises One Hundred Twenty-Three through One Hundred Thirty-Three contain all the notes we have learned. Because we are using a Movable Do System, you may begin singing with any pitch that feels comfortable.

Each exercise is to be sung at least twice each day. The first time, the scale degree number (1, 2, 3, 4, 5, 6, 7) is to be sung. The second time, the syllable (Do, Re, Mi, Fa, Sol, La, Ti) is to be sung.

Each week's lesson should be comprised of as many exercises as can be comfortably absorbed.

Do not play any exercise on a musical instrument before first singing it. When necessary, a musical instrument or a pitch pipe may be used to check for accuracy.

Take a breath whenever it is comfortable to do so. All of the sight singing exercises are to be sung legato.

Think the sound of each note before you sing it.

SIGHT SINGING EXERCISES 123 THROUGH 133

LET'S LEARN TO SIGHT SING IN THE KEY OF F MAJOR

SIGHT SINGING THE F MAJOR SCALE AND ITS EXTENSIONS

The notes of the F Major scale are F, G, A, Bb, C, D, E, and F. As with all Major Scales, the ascending degrees of the scale are numbered 1, 2, 3, 4, 5, 6, 7, and 1. The degrees of the scale are sung with the syllables Do, Re, Mi, Fa, Sol, La, Ti, Do.

The interval from F to G is a MAJOR SECOND.
The interval from G to A is a MAJOR SECOND.
The interval from Bb to C is a MAJOR SECOND.
The interval from C to D is a MAJOR SECOND.
The interval from D to E is a MAJOR SECOND.
The interval from A to Bb is a MINOR SECOND.
The interval from E to F is a MINOR SECOND.
The interval from F to A is a MAJOR THIRD.
The interval from Bb to D is a MAJOR THIRD.
The interval from C to E is a MAJOR THIRD.
The interval from G to Bb is a MINOR THIRD.
The interval from A to C is a MINOR THIRD.
The interval from D to F is a MINOR THIRD.
The interval from F to Bb is a PERFECT FOURTH.
The interval from G to C is a PERFECT FOURTH.
The interval from A to D is a PERFECT FOURTH.
The interval from C to F is a PERFECT FOURTH.
The interval from Bb to E is an AUGMENTED FOURTH.
The interval from F to C is a PERFECT FIFTH.
The interval from G to D is a PERFECT FIFTH.
The interval from A to E is a PERFECT FIFTH.
The interval from Bb to F is a PERFECT FIFTH.
The interval from F to D is a MAJOR SIXTH.
The interval from G to E is a MAJOR SIXTH.
The interval from A to F is a MINOR SIXTH.
The interval from F to E is a MAJOR SEVENTH.
The interval from G to F is a MINOR SEVENTH.
The interval from F to F is a PERFECT OCTAVE.

Exercises One Hundred Thirty-Four through One Hundred Sixty-Four contain the notes that comprise the Key of F Major. Because we are using a Movable Do System, you may begin singing with any pitch that feels comfortable.

If notes should occur which are too high or too low to be comfortably accommodated by the vocal range, the student is to "think" the notes (sing the notes in the mind) rather than sing the notes aloud. If convenient, the student may lower or raise troublesome passages an octave to bring them within the vocal range.

Each exercise is to be sung at least twice each day. The first time, the scale degree number (1, 2, 3, 4, 5, 6, 7) is to be sung. The second time, the syllable (Do, Re, Mi, Fa, Sol, La, Ti) is to be sung.

Each week's lesson should be comprised of as many exercises as can be comfortably absorbed.

Do not play any exercise on a musical instrument before first singing it. When necessary, a musical instrument or a pitch pipe may be used to check for accuracy.

Take a breath whenever it is comfortable to do so. All of the sight singing exercises are to be sung legato.

Think the sound of each note before you sing it.

Sing softly and without strain.

SIGHT SINGING EXERCISES 134 THROUGH 144

SIGHT SINGING EXERCISES 145 THROUGH 156

SIGHT SINGING EXERCISES 157 THROUGH 164

ADDITIONAL ASSIGNMENTS

For additional sight singing practice in other keys, the student should transpose the preceding exercises.

Using manuscript paper, transpose Exercises One through Sixty-Seven from the Key of C Major to the Key of Bb Major. The student should then practice sight singing the transposed exercises. When this has been completed, Exercises Sixty-Eight through One Hundred Thirty-Three are to be transposed from the Key of G Major to the Key of Ab Major. The student is to practice sight singing these transposed exercises. Finally, Exercises One Hundred Thirty-Four through One Hundred Sixty-Four are to be transposed from the Key of F Major to the Key of Eb Major. These, too, are to be used for sight singing practice.

The transposed sight singing exercises are to be practiced in the same manner as the original sight singing exercises. Each week's practice should be comprised of as many exercises as can be comfortably absorbed. Better too few exercises than too many.

SINGING ACCIDENTALS

An ACCIDENTAL is a chromatic sign (sharp, flat, natural) not appearing in the key signature, which occurs before a note in a composition. While a sharp or flat in the key signature is applied throughout the piece, an accidental affects only those notes within its measure which follow on the same line or space of the staff.

In the Movable Do System, accidentals are accommodated by changing the syllable for the sharped or flatted note.

The sharped 1st degree of the scale is sung Di (pronounced *dee*).
The sharped 2nd degree of the scale is sung Ri (pronounced *ree*).
The sharped 4th degree of the scale is sung Fi (pronounced *fee*).
The sharped 5th degree of the scale is sung Si (pronounced *see*).
The sharped 6th degree of the scale is sung Li (pronounced *lee*).

The flatted 2nd degree of the scale is sung Rah (pronounced *rah*).
The flatted 3rd degree of the scale is sung Me (pronounced *may*).
The flatted 5th degree of the scale is sung Se (pronounced *say*).
The flatted 6th degree of the scale is sung Le (pronounced *lay*).
The flatted 7th degree of the scale is sung Te (pronounced *tay*).

There is considerable disagreement among teachers of sight singing with regard to the proper pronunciation of the syllables. However, if Do is pronounced "dough" or "dew," or if Se is pronounced "saw" or "say," it has no bearing upon the process of learning to sight sing or the performance of sight singing. The pronunciations presented above are accepted by many experts. Deviations from these pronunciations may be equally correct.

MODULATION

Whereas TRANSPOSITION is the act of performing or writing a composition in a key other than the original, MODULATION is the act of passing from one key to another. It is not uncommon for a selection to modulate several times before it is completed.

Because the posting of a new key signature each time a melody modulates would tend to complicate the appearance of printed music, it is customary to effect changes of key within a song by the use of chromatic signs.

Examples of well known songs that modulate are *Winter Wonderland, Satin Doll,* and *Tea for Two.*

The example below, if sung with the syllables representing sharps, would be quite difficult. However, by being aware of the key change and by recognizing the new tonic as Do, and the other notes of the scale as being syllabized accordingly, the act of sight singing the two measures in the Key of C# Major becomes very simple.

MINOR SCALES

For each Major scale there is a minor scale which is related. The two scales are related because they share the same key signature and contain the same notes.

Despite these similarities, the Major scale and its relative minor are totally different scales because they have different tonics.

On the other hand, major and minor scales with the same tonic share a common tonality. Major and minor scales with the same tonic are called PARALLEL MAJOR and MINOR SCALES. Examples are C Major and C minor, D Major and D minor.

Each Major scale may be changed into its parallel minor scale by lowering the third and sixth degrees one half tone. To change the scale of C Major to the scale of C (harmonic) minor, the E is lowered to Eb, and the A is lowered to Ab.

C Major Scale =	C	D	E	F	G	A	B	C
	1	2	3	4	5	6	7	8
C minor Scale =	C	D	Eb	F	G	Ab	B	C
	1	2	3b	4	5	6b	7	8

In the same manner that a Major scale may be changed to a minor scale by lowering the third and sixth degrees one half step, a song may be changed from major to minor by lowering all third and sixth degree notes one half tone.

SIGHT SINGING IN A MINOR KEY

The 1st degree of the scale is sung Do (pronounced *dough*).
The 2nd degree of the scale is sung Re (pronounced *ray*).
The 3rd degree of the scale is sung Me (pronounced *may*).
The 4th degree of the scale is sung Fa (pronounced *fah*).
The 5th degree of the scale is sung Sol (pronounced *so*).
The 6th degree of the scale is sung Le (pronounced *lay*).
The 7th degree of the scale is sung Ti (pronounced *tee*).

SECTION FOUR

DELIVERY TECHNIQUE AND SHAPING A SONG FOR PERFORMANCE

The function of the voice teacher is to develop the singer's tone, range and ability to sing in tune (intonation). The vocal coach teaches the pupil how to apply a properly developed voice to singing songs. Very frequently the voice teacher also acts as a vocal coach.

Vocal coaches are of two types, the concert or opera coach and the popular song coach. The opera coach specializes in the performance of operatic selections or concert pieces. The popular song coach teaches the student how to deliver and shape a popular song for performance. The term "POPULAR SONG" refers to all types of contemporary music, from show tunes to rock to jazz.

This section is concerned with delivery technique, *i.e.,* the information necessary to sing popular songs properly. Delivery technique is at least as important as a well-developed voice for, though a singer may possess a magnificent voice, broad vocal range and perfect intonation, if delivery technique is lacking, the performance of a popular song will be blatantly amateurish.

Listen, Listen, Listen

The vocal student must not live in a vacuum. Exposure to all styles of music performed by various singers and musicians is vital to development of delivery technique. When listening to singers, observe their pronunciation. Notice how they join words into phrases. Listen to their vocal tricks and mannerisms. Pay special attention to their alteration of the song melody, and to the way they abbreviate or extend notes beyond their given time values. Listen, Listen, Listen. Be influenced by all that you hear, but never, never attempt to copy style or to impersonate a voice.

Sing, Sing, Sing

Another element that is vital toward development as a singer is the singing of popular songs as much as time permits. Sing in the bath and shower. Sing while driving the car. Sing while walking the dog. Sing while washing the dishes. Sing slow tunes, fast tunes, sing softly, moderately, loudly (but never strain), sing sad songs, sing happy songs, and then sing some more.

Singing in front of an audience will provide the opportunity to overcome self-consciousness and to gain confidence, but should be attempted only when your teacher or a musician upon whose judgment you can rely assures you that you are ready.

PRACTICE IN FRONT OF A MIRROR

A pleasant facial expression is not only beneficial for the production of a good vocal tone, but is essential for bridging the gap between the performer and the audience.

Frequently the singer may develop unpleasant facial characteristics, especially when singing notes on the high or low end of the vocal range. Usually the singer is unaware of unappealing mannerisms which creep into the performance.

The best way to avoid undesirable expressions or gestures is by occasional practice in front of a full-length mirror.

A SPECIAL NOTE TO OPERA SINGERS

When used for classical singing, the voice is a beautiful instrument. But the rendering of popular music with a classical delivery style is simply awful.

To avoid slipping into classical mannerisms when performing a popular song, the opera singer should choose the lowest practical key, use vibrato sparingly, and should sing at a volume level considerably lower than that employed for concert selections. Also, remember that popular singing, except for jazz effects, does not permit a crescendo within a word.

SINCERITY IS AN IMPORTANT INGREDIENT

The vocalist singing "I love you" must not leave any doubt of his sincerity. The young woman describing in song how she was cast aside by her lover should evoke compassion from her audience. However, the words that roll so easily off the lips of the skilled singer are often the result of hours of practice devoted to perfecting delivery technique. The finished product should be natural and honest. And there should not be the slightest trace of affectation.

PREPARING A SONG FOR PERFORMANCE

THE MELODY

The initial step in preparing a song for performance is to memorize the melody. If one plays an instrument, this is accomplished by repeatedly playing the melody. Or, the record or cassette of the song should be played until the melody is committed to memory. If the vocalist can sight sing, the sheet music or manuscript is to be studied until every note is secure.

When singing the melody at this point, the words are not to be sung. Instead, use syllables such as lah, dah, dee, dum, doo, etc. Practice singing the melody in the key that feels most comfortable.

THE LYRICS

Read the lyrics to yourself a few times to determine the song's message. Is the song sad, happy, thoughtful? Next, read the lyrics aloud, speaking them as you would in conversation. The lyrics are to be spoken naturally, with no affectations, no unnatural accent, no imitation of your favorite singer... only a normal conversational manner of speech is to be employed.

After the lyrics have been read silently, analyzed for content and read aloud, the next step is to memorize them exactly as you would speak them in normal conversation. Finally, the lyrics are to be applied to the melody of the song.

When telling a funny story, you smile. When relating a tragedy, you appear sad. However, if you smile when describing a tragedy, your listener would believe you to be extremely cruel, or else mildly retarded. Your singing voice and manner should reflect the mood of the lyrics you are singing.

At this time you are to select the key and tempo for performance of the song. You will notice that the key you choose may differ from the key you selected for syllabizing the melody.

As the song is being learned, special attention should be paid to singing in tune (intonation). A melody that is sung with poor intonation is as unnerving to the audience as the beginning violin student who plays his instrument out of tune.

PHRASING AND BREATHING

The Lyric Phrase

A lyric phrase is ended and a new phrase is begun at each pause that occurs in normal conversation. As in conversation, a breath need not necessarily be taken at the beginning of each lyric phrase. Simply by observing the manner in which we normally speak and most naturally sing, breathing while singing is as trouble-free as breathing while speaking.

The Melodic Phrase

Melodic phrases are ended and new phrases begun at the pauses that occur in the song melody.

Frequently a song's melodic phrases and lyic phrases occur together. When the melodic phrase and the lyric phrase do not coincide, THE LYRIC PHRASE ALWAYS RECEIVES PREFERENCE.

If the song melody forces the lyric phrase to differ from conversational speech, the note values must be extended or abbreviated so that the lyric becomes conversational. This is to be done without altering the meter of the song.

METER

Meter refers to the number of beats appearing in each measure. For example, music in 3/4 time contains three beats in each measure. To alter the meter (by singing out of meter) means to perform the notes and rests comprising a measure in either less than or more than three beats.

In other words, if you should sing the words that occur in a measure, in either the preceding measure or the following measure, you are probably (though not necessarily) singing out of meter. Music that is sung out of meter is always dreadfully incorrect. There is never an exception to this rule.

However, within any given measure the singer may extend notes and abbreviate notes, provided that the total time required to perform the measure does not extend beyond or fall short of the required number of beats (3 beats in 3/4 time, 4 beats in 4/4 time, etc.). This altering of time values is frequently necessary to make the lyric phrase conversational and to render an interesting performance.

CHANGING THE MELODY

To make a word or phrase easier to sing, to add interest to a second chorus, to tailor a song to your style, or to provide a modern ending, the notes of a song may be changed.

If a single note or an entire phrase is either too high or too low to be sung comfortably, the solution may be as simple as lowering or raising the troublesome notes an octave.

At times, changing octaves does not provide the desired result. Another approach is to replace the troublesome notes with others that are derived from the chord harmony (accompaniment chord). For a better understanding of the application of melody substitution, listen to professional singers as they change song melodies. Experiment with melody substitution whenever a song's passage feels awkward or strained.

SINGING DICTION

Singing diction is much like conversational diction, but in song, the melody may require some syllables to be sustained for an unusually long period. To compound the singer's problem, some speech sounds cannot be sustained at all. Examples are the "t" in "telephone," the "b" in "boy," the "p" in "pipe." If the melody demands that these or any of the other consonants be sustained, the singer must be able to respond properly to the demands of the music.

To solve diction problems, it is necessary to become familiar with vowels, consonants, and diphthongs.

Vowels are vocal sounds that can be sustained (sung). They are sounds based upon the letters A, E, I, O, U. At times the letter Y is treated as a vowel. For example, the word "you" is sung *ee-you,* or the word "yellow" is sung *ee-eh-low.*

Consonants are all vocal sounds other than vowels. Consonants have no time value, and therefore cannot be sustained (sung).

If the melody suggests that a consonant be sustained, then the consonant is passed over quickly and a more attractive neighboring sound is sustained. For example, in the word "heart" only the "ah" sound is easily sung. The correct way to sing "heart" is *hah.......rt.* Improper singing diction is *hahr.......t.*

THE DIPHTHONG *(DIF-thong* or *DIP-thong)*

A diphthong is a speech sound that begins with a vowel sound and moves to another vowel sound within the same syllable. In the word "oil," the diphthong is pronounced *aw-ee.* In the word "out," the diphthong is pronounced *ah-oo.* Other diphthongs are found in "day" *(eh-ee),* "dough" *(ow-oo),* "fair" *(eh-uh).*

When singing diphthongs, the initial sound is sustained for almost the total time value of the note (or notes). The final sound, which is called the "vanish," is sung briefly.

DOUBLE VOWELS

With the exception of the letter "e," each vowel sound is pronounced so that it has two sounds: "a" = *eh-ee,* "i" = *ah-ee,* "o" = *oh-oo,* "u" = *ee-oo.*

Vowels which are pronounced so that they have two vowel sounds are called "double vowels." The double vowel behaves exactly like a diphthong. The double vowel "i" in the word "night" is pronounced *ah-ee.* In the word "no," the double vowel "o" is pronounced *oh-oo.*

The final vowel sound of a double vowel is called "the vanish." When singing the double vowels A, I, O, the initial sound is sustained for almost the total time value of the note (or notes). The vanish is sung briefly at the conclusion of the note. For example, the proper manner for singing the word "day" is *deh.......ee.* Improper singing diction is *deh-ee.......ee.*

An exception to the rule is the double vowel U, in which the initial sound is very short and the final sound is sustained. The word "use" should be sung *ee-oo.......s.*

Rules are needed for the singing of double vowels and diphthongs because they contain two vowel sounds, one of which is more attractive than the other. Singing diction rules tell us to sustain the attractive vowel sound and to abbreviate the less appealing sound. The longer a note is sustained—especially at a slow tempo—the more important the rule becomes. If the melody requires that the word "mine" is to be sustained, especially on a high note, there is no doubt that *mah.......een* is more appealing than *mah-ee.......n.*

CARELESS DICTION

Careless diction occurs so frequently in normal conversation that we are usually unaware when we hear "later tonight" as "later t'night," or "young and lovely" as "young 'n' lovely," or "I want you" as "I wanchoo," or "in other words" as " 'nother words," or "I didn't want to hurt you" as "I didn' wanna herchoo."

Careless diction is a serious fault, often committed by inexperienced singers. While the vocalist may delude himself into believing that sloppy diction appears natural and casual, the audience perceives it to be unprofessional and unappealing.

A GOOD RULE TO REMEMBER

Sustaining a syllable in song is the same as accenting a syllable in speech. Therefore, sustain only those syllables that are normally accented in conversation.

A FREQUENTLY MISPRONOUNCED WORD

A frequently mispronounced word is "BEAUTIFUL." This word is to be sung with the same diction as when it is spoken. It should never be sung "beauteeee...ful." There should be no "e" sound when speaking or singing "BEAUTIFUL."

CONSONANTS WHICH MAY BE SUSTAINED

It was mentioned earlier that vowels are to be sung and consonants are to be pronounced as quickly as possible. However, an exception to this rule may be applied to the letters "L," "M," and "N." It is at times acceptable to sustain the humming sound of "M" and "N." For example, "man" can be sung *maaaannnn* or *mmmmmaaannnn.* The letter "L" can also be sustained at times. For example, the word "love" can be sung *llllluh....... v.*

HYPHENATED WORDS

Very frequently, words of the lyric are hyphenated. The word "stagger" may appear as "stag-ger." To sing this word as written would be a serious error in vocal diction. A proper approach is to sing the word as *staaa-ger.* The hyphen is shifted from one part of the word to another for a more appealing delivery.

WORDS THAT CONTAIN "R"

Of considerable difficulty to the inexperienced singer are words that contain the sound "R." Because the "R" sound is unattractive when sung, the more attractive neighboring vowel is to be sustained while the "R" is passed over quickly. For example, "are" is sung *ah.... r,* "bird" is sung *buh.... rd,* "word" is sung *wuh.... rd,* "fur" is sung *fuh.... r,* "girl" is sung *guh.... rl,* "work" is sung *wuh.... rk,* "burn" is sung *buh.... rn,* etc. Bear in mind that all word pronunciations should sound natural.

BUILDING A REPERTOIRE

At first the pupil should devote all repertoire practice time to learning a single song. When this has been accomplished to a reasonable degree, the pupil should attempt to learn and memorize two songs at the same time while continuing to review the first song. The next step is to work on three new songs while reviewing the previously learned songs. With the passage of time and practice, the student will find that far less effort and time are required to learn new songs. And even if only one song is learned each week, over a period of a year the student will know over fifty songs. Though it is difficult to establish how many songs are required for professional performance, it is safe to say that at least fifty songs should be memorized and polished.

THE ACCOMPANIST

The singer who does not play an accompanying instrument must practice repertoire without accompaniment, or else must bear the expense of engaging a musician.

When rehearsing with an accompanist, each session should be as fruitful as possible. Rehearsal time should be devoted to polishing for performance the songs that have already been learned. Generally, it is unwise to devote expensive rehearsal time to practicing (learning songs).

Often, the accompanist will make suggestions that can improve the delivery of a song. As part of the learning process, the singer should experience working with various accompanists.

ESTABLISHING THE VOCAL KEY DURING PERFORMANCE

During a performance the singer is "given" the key when the accompanist plays a dominant seventh chord or arpeggio, with the root of the chord as the highest pitched chord note, or with the root of the chord as the final note of the arpeggio.

The dominant seventh chord is built upon the fifth note of the scale of the key in which the selection is to be sung.

For example, if the melody is in the key of C Major, the fifth note of the C Major scale is "G; the accompanist plays the G Seventh chord or arpeggiated chord as a lead in to the key of C Major. If the selection is in the Key of F Major, the fifth note of the F Major scale is "C"; the accompanist plays the C Seventh chord or arpeggiated chord as a lead in to the key. For the Key of G Major, the D Seventh chord is played. For the Key of Bb Major, the F Seventh chord is played.

The dominant seventh chord as a lead in to the song is the most preferred and in greatest use. If the singer prefers to hear the key note or starting note of the song, this must be prearranged.

AD LIB AND IN TEMPO

If the vocalist is required to sing for dancers, the music is performed "in tempo." This means that the beat of the music is steady and even, without growing slower or faster.

Ad Lib style provides for variations in volume and tempo in performing a selection. Ad Lib style is fine for a nightclub act or any performance where dancing does not take place. The singer should be equipped to sing in either style.

CHORD SYMBOLS

As we have learned in music theory, each chord is given a name, such as G Major, C Major, D Dominant Seventh, G Dominant Seventh, A minor, D minor, etc. The musician and singer refer to the chord name as a "CHORD SYMBOL."

In written music, all Major chords are indicated by their letter name only. Therefore, G Major is called "G," C Major is called "C," etc.

Dominant Seventh chords appear as their letter name followed by the number "7," such as D7, G7, etc.

Minor chords are shown by their letter name followed by the small letter "m," such as Am, Dm, etc.

THE LEAD SHEET (rhymes with NEED)

The singer frequently comes across the term "LEAD SHEET." The lead sheet consists of one or more sheets of music which contain the song melody, lyrics, and chord symbols. The chord symbols represent the harmony or accompaniment chords for the song.

IN CLOSING

Acquiring a beautiful voice requires time, effort and patience. By faithfully following the instructions and suggestions appearing in this volume, you will accomplish your objective.

Good luck with the successful development of a wonderful singing voice.

APPENDIX

CLASSIFICATION OF VOICES

Vocal tonal qualities differ from one person to the next, as do eye coloring, height, shape of the head, etc.

The variations of vocal tone quality are influenced by differences in vocal cords and resonating chambers, by age (children and adults), and by sex.

The female voice is divided into two main categories. The soprano is the higher pitched, and the contralto the lower.

Soprano voices are classified as:
- **Lyric Soprano**—Light, high, flute-like quality.
- **Dramatic Soprano**—Powerful voice, heavy quality, histrionic ability.
- **Coloratura Soprano**—Great agility, high range, flexible, able to warble (trill) rapidly.
- **Mezzo-Soprano**—Possesses the qualities of both the soprano and the contralto.

The Contralto voice is the lowest pitched female voice. In the present terminology the words "contralto" and "alto" have the same meaning.

The voice of a young girl may be either contralto or soprano. Also, the voice of a young boy may be either contralto or soprano.

The adult male voice is divided into three categories. The tenor is the highest of the three. The baritone is the mid-range male voice. The bass is the lowest pitched male voice.

Tenor voices are classified as:
- **Lyric Tenor**—Also called Tenore Leggiero, light, high, corresponding to the Lyric Soprano.
- **Spinto Tenor**—Possessing the light quality of the Lyric Tenor, but capable of the power needed for dramatic climaxes.
- **Dramatic Tenor**—Also called Tenore Robusto, full voice and the power necessary for strong passion.
- **Heldentenor**—Literally "hero-tenor," the same as Tenore Robusto, a big-voiced tenor, suitable for heavy operatic parts.

The Baritone voice is lower than Tenor and higher than Bass.

Bass voices are classified as:
- **Basso Cantante**—A Bass voice with qualities of both the Bass and the Baritone. A Bass Baritone.
- **Basso Profundo**—Deep Bass, low range and powerful, capable of deep solemn expression.

Voice classification is determined primarily by the quality of the voice and not by the range. However, as a rough guide to vocal classification by range, the following is presented.

Vocal parts appearing in sheet music are always written in the treble clef. The actual pitch of the female voice is the same as that of the notes appearing on the printed page.

The actual pitch of the male voice is one octave lower than the notes appearing on the printed page.

THE FALSETTO VOICE

The falsetto voice is an unnatural high-pitched male voice that lies above the natural range. It begins where the natural voice leaves off, and lacks the warm overtones that are found in the normal male vocal range. The sound of the falsetto voice is not unlike that of the normal (and relatively rare) adult male alto or soprano.

The falsetto quality is produced by vibration at the edges of the vocal cords, with the larynx held in a high position.

THE CASTRATO VOICE

During the seventeenth and eighteenth centuries, many well-meaning but ignorant parents subjected their male children to castration in order to halt the development of their vocal cords. Because of the demand for the adult male soprano or contralto voice, the parents of the castrated young boys envisioned a future of fame and fortune for their offspring. Unfortunately castration also prevents the development of male characteristics. To further compound the tragedy, the majority of the castrated boys had no exceptional musical or vocal talent, nor did they have the slightest chance for success as a castrato singer.

At that time, the castrato voice was so popular that there was a surprising disinterest in the natural male voice. There were even performances of operas in which all of the male singers were castrati. As an example of the popularity of this surgically created voice, Handel's friend Mattheson, writing of the years when they were associated in the Hamburg Opera House (1703-1706) says, "At that time, no man was called a great singer unless he had this sort of voice." The last of the castratti were Velluti (1781-1861), who was heard in London in 1820, and Pergetti, who was heard in London as late as 1844.

The most famous castrato singer who ever lived was Farinelli (1705-1782), who spent a quarter of a century at the Court of Spain and, during the last ten years of the lifetime of Philip V, sang to him every evening the same four songs and nothing else.

The practice of castration to produce castrati was abolished by Napoleon, but it continued in Italy to the end of the nineteenth century, if not later.

UNUSUAL VOICES

The Male Alto and Male Soprano are unusual voices that are high-pitched and lacking in the qualities that are associated with the male voice. The Male Alto and the Male Soprano voice are extremely rare.

THE CHANGING MALE VOICE AT PUBERTY

It is usual at puberty for a boy's voice to be somewhat uncontrollable for a period of time, due to the sudden and unequal growth of the vocal cords and the associated ligaments and muscles. It then settles into a voice that is approximately one octave lower.

During the time that the voice is in the process of changing, no harm will come to the voice if the boy continues to sing without strain or force. However, if the voice changes very quickly and drastically and is constantly cracking, it may be wise to suspend singing temporarily until the adult voice, with some measure of control, has been attained.

FREAK VOICES

Freak voices sometimes occur, such as women tenors. In 1936, there was broadcast from Prague the singing of a boy of three who possessed a deep bass voice.

The separate classifications for "unusual voices" and "freak voices" are due to the public acceptance of the abnormally high-pitched male voice, while frowning upon a deep, masculine-sounding female voice. Beginning with the 1950s, there have been many male singers in the contemporary popular field who gained considerable success with unusually high-pitched voices. Two notable examples are Neil Sedaka and Michael Jackson.

MOST COMMON VOICES

The most common voices are the Mezzo-Soprano and the Baritone. Nature has created many of them and relatively few of the others.

MICROPHONE TECHNIQUE

A microphone is a transducer. A transducer is a device that converts energy of one form into energy of another form. The microphone converts acoustical (sound) energy into electrical energy. The electrical energy produced by the microphone goes through what is called a "sound chain." The sound chain is comprised of the sound source (voice or musical instrument) to the microphone, to the microphone mixer, to the amplifier, to the loudspeaker. At times the sound chain excludes the mixer stage.

A microphone that accepts sound equally well from all sides is called an "omnidirectional microphone." An omnidirectional microphone is very effective for covering a vocal group standing around the microphone. A disadvantage of the omnidirectional microphone is its tendency to feedback.

Feedback is an annoying howl or squeal that can be avoided by altering the position of the microphone, reducing the volume or by altering the settings of the tone control.

A unidirectional microphone, often referred to as a cardioid microphone, accepts sound mostly from one direction—in front—while reducing the pickup of sounds from the sides and rear. The unidirectional microphone will tend to reject feedback. Of importance to the singer is that most unidirectional microphones boost the bass when used up close, an effect that adds robustness to a thin voice. This is called the "proximity effect."

Each room provides a different tonal balance. Place the microphone at various distances from the lips until you arrive at the desired tone quality. If necessary, adjust the amplifier for more or less bass, or more or less treble, depending upon the way you would like your voice to be reproduced.

Place the microphone only as close as necessary. Miking too close can color the quality of the voice to an unpleasant degree.

To reduce "pop" (the explosive breath sounds that occur with the letters "P," "B," and "T"), mike either closer or further than three inches from the mouth. This is because at the three-inch distance the "pop" is maximized. Other ways to reduce "pop" are to place the microphone to the side, above, or below the mouth; or use an omnidirectional microphone; or use a microphone with a pop filter. The pop filter can be an external foam windscreen that is slipped over the microphone.

The microphone is the singer's best friend. If possible, practice performing with a microphone from time to time to become familiar with the positioning and angling necessary to provide the best results for your voice.

MUSIC TERMINOLOGY

The motorist driving along unfamiliar highways may take a wrong turn and find himself utterly lost unless he is able to read the road signs along the way. In much the same manner, the singer who does not follow the musical directions which appear in a selection will quickly stray from the musical interpretation intended by the composer or arranger.

The musical terms which follow are extremely important. The student should memorize all of them. To insure retention of all terms, abbreviations and signs, the student should periodically return to these pages to refresh his memory.

TEMPO DESIGNATIONS

THE FOLLOWING TEMPO TERMS INDICATE A SPECIFIC RATE OF SPEED.

Andante *(on-DON-tay):* Leisurely but not too slow.
Moderato *(mod-a-RAH-toe):* Moderately, at a moderate tempo.
Allegro *(al-LAY-grow):* Merry, quick, lively, bright.
Adagio *(a-DAH-jee-o):* At ease, tranquil, slower than Andante.
Lento *(LEN-toe):* Slow.
Largo *(LARR-go):* Large, broad, dignified, slow and stately movement.
Andantino *(on-don-TEE-no):* This word is a diminutive of Andante, and means "a little slower than Andante." However, it is often used as if meaning "a little faster than Andante." Upon coming across this ambiguous term, a performer must use his judgment. It is advisable for composers and arrangers to avoid this confusing term.
Allegretto *(al-lay-GRET-toe):* Light and cheerful, but not as much as Allegro. A little slower than Allegro.

VARIATIONS IN TEMPO

THE FOLLOWING TEMPO TERMS INDICATE A CHANGE OF SPEED. USUALLY THEY APPEAR BELOW THE STAFF AND ARE WRITTEN AS AN ABBREVIATION.

Accelerando *(ac-sell-ay-RON-doe)* or *(at-shell-ay-RON-doe)* (Abbreviation is *accel.*): Gradually accelerate the tempo.
Ritardando *(ree-tar-DON-doe)* (Abbreviation is *rit.* or *ritard.*):
Ritardo *(ree-TAHR-doe)* (Abbreviation is *rit.* or *ritard.*):
Rallentando *(ral-len-TAHN-doe)* (Abbreviation is *rall.*):
} Gradually slow down.
Piu mosso *(PEW MOSS-soh):* More movement. To be played at a steady rate of speed, but faster than that which preceded.
Piu moto *(PEW MAW-toe):* Same as *piu mosso,* above.

Meno mosso *(MAY-no MOSS-soh):* Less movement. To be played at a steady rate of speed, but slower than that which preceded.
Meno moto *(MAY-no MAW-toe):* Same as *meno mosso,* above.
A Tempo *(ah TEM-poe):* Indicates a return to the original speed after a brief change of tempo.

DYNAMIC SYMBOLS

VARYING DEGREES OF LOUDNESS (VOLUME) WITHIN A COMPOSITION ARE CALLED DYNAMICS. THE LETTERS, TERMS, SIGNS AND ABBREVIATIONS USED TO DESCRIBE THE DYNAMICS OF A COMPOSITION ARE CALLED DYNAMIC SYMBOLS.

LETTERS DESIGNATING VOLUME LEVELS

Piano *(pee-AH-no)*	***p***	Soft.
Forte *(FOR-tay)*	***f***	Loud.
Mezzo Piano *(MET-so pee-AH-no)*	***mp***	Moderately soft. A little louder than "Piano."
Mezzo Forte *(MET-so FOR-tay)*	***mf***	Moderately loud. A little softer than "Forte."
Pianissimo *(pee-an-EESS-see-moe)*	***pp***	Very soft.
Fortissimo *(for-TEESS-see-moe)*	***ff***	Very loud.

A volume level that is softer than pianissimo (***pp***) is indicated by the addition of ***p***. For example, ***ppp*** ***pppp***

A volume level that is louder than fortissimo (***ff***) is indicated by the addition of ***f***. For example, ***fff*** ***ffff***

TERMS SIGNIFYING A CHANGE OF VOLUME

Crescendo *(cray-SHEN-doe)* (Abbreviation is *cresc.* or *cres.*): Gradually grow louder.
Decrescendo *(dee-cray-SHEN-doe)* (Abbreviation is *decresc.*):
Diminuendo *(dee-min-you-EN-doe)* (Abbreviation is *dim.*):
} Gradually grow softer.

SIGNS REPRESENTING A CHANGE OF VOLUME

Gradually grow louder.

Gradually grow softer.

INTERPRETATION SIGNS

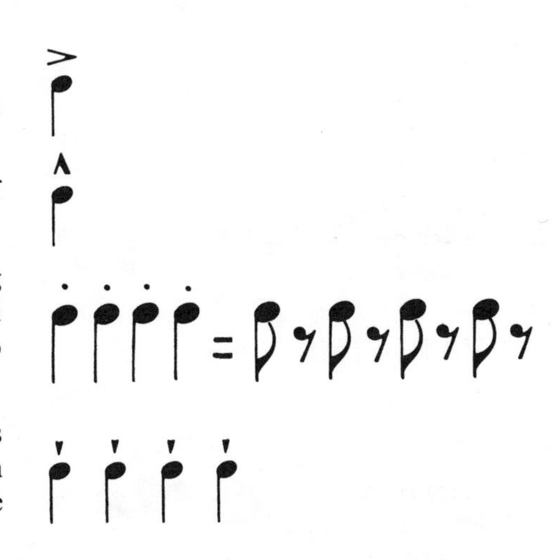

The Accent: When a note or chord is to receive a special emphasis, an ACCENT MARK is placed above or below it.

Sometimes the accent mark appears vertically instead of horizontally.

The Staccato *(stac-CAH-toe):* From the Italian word meaning "separated." A dot appearing above or below a note or chord indicates that it is to be played in a short detached manner, so that its time value is shortened by approximately one half.

The staccatissimo *(stac-cat-EESS-see-moh)*: If pointed wedges occur above or below a note or chord, more shortening (than staccato) is required, so that it receives approximately one fourth of its written value.

GLOSSARY OF VOCAL ORGANS

ARYTENOID CARTILAGES: (See cartilages.)

CARTILAGES: The framework of the larynx. The largest cartilage is the Thyroid Cartilage, whose bulge creates the Adam's Apple. The Cricoid Cartilage is a structural part of the larynx, and is attached to the trachea. The Arytenoid Cartilages are responsible for adjusting tension and the amount of separation of the vocal cords. The vocal cords are attached to the Arytenoid Cartilages at the back and to the Thyroid Cartilage at the front.

CLAVICLE: The collarbone.

CLAVICULAR BREATHING: Characterized by an upward heaving of the chest.

COSTAL: Pertaining to the ribs.

COSTAL BREATHING: Breathing involving movement of the ribs, as distinct from movements of the diaphragm.

CRICOID: (See cartilages.)

DIAPHRAGM: The flexible partition of muscles and tendons separating the chest and abdominal cavities.

EPIGLOTTIS: The cartilage at the root of the tongue, which during swallowing covers and protects the vocal cords.

GLOTTIS: The space between the vocal cords.

HYOID BONE: The bone at the base of the tongue, to which both tongue and larynx have attachments.

LARYNX: The voice box. The cavity holding the vocal cords.

PALATE: The roof of the mouth. The front is called the Hard Palate. The back is called the Soft Palate.

PHARYNX: The throat. The cavity connecting the nose, mouth and larynx.

SINUSES: Small bony cavities in the skull.

STERNUM: The breast bone, to which the fronts of the upper ribs are attached.

THORAX: The upper part of the body between the neck and the abdomen. Separated from the abdomen by the diaphragm.

TRACHEA: The windpipe. The air passage leading into the larynx from below.

UVULA: The fleshy, hanging projection at the back of the soft palate.